"The plays of Young Jean Lee are as personal and probing as they are utterly demented."

—*New Yorker*

"Miss Lee has a talent for evocative and sometimes grotesque imagery, and on the attack she is at the height of her powers."

—*New York Times*

"Lee is building a jittery, jagged body of work that resists pat definition—except as emotionally raw dispatches from an angry mind that lacerates itself as much as it does the world."

—*TimeOut New York*

"Lee is a queen of unease; chuckles never come unaccompanied by squirms."

—*Village Voice*

"The clearest indication that the avant-garde isn't dead, and has never been funnier."

—*New York*

"A rising star of the downtown theater scene."

—*New York Times*

"Lee confirms herself as one of the best experimental playwrights in America."

—*TimeOut New York*

Songs of the Dragons
Flying to Heaven
and Other Plays

Songs of the Dragons Flying to Heaven and Other Plays

Young Jean Lee

Theatre Communications Group   New York   2009

Songs of the Dragons Flying to Heaven and Other Plays is published by Theatre Communications Group, Inc., 520 Eighth Avenue, 24th Floor, New York, NY 10018-4156

This publication is made possible in part with public funds from the New York State Council on the Arts, a State Agency.

TCG books are exclusively distributed to the book trade by Consortium Book Sales and Distribution.

LIBRARY OF CONGRESS CATALOGING-IN-PUBLICATION DATA
Lee, Young Jean.
Songs of the dragons flying to heaven and other plays / Young Jean Lee.
—1st ed.
p. cm.
ISBN 978-1-55936-326-6
I. Title.
PS3612.E228S66   2008
811'.6—dc22   2008050891

Book design, cover design and composition by Lisa Govan
Cover art by Jesse Hawley

First Edition, April 2009

For my father
James M. Lee

Contents

Church

For my mother
Inn-Soo Lee

Production History

Church was originally produced by Young Jean Lee's Theater Company. It premiered in April 2007 at Performance Space 122 in New York. It was directed by Young Jean Lee; the set was by Eric Dyer, the lighting design was by Mark Barton, the costume design was by Normandy Sherwood, the sound design was by Matthew Tierney and the choreography was by Faye Driscoll. It was performed by:

REVEREND JOSÉ	Greg Hildreth
REVEREND KARINNE	Karinne Keithley
REVEREND WEENA	Weena Pauly
REVEREND KATIE	Katie Workum
CHOIR DIRECTOR	Anna Shapiro
SOLOIST	Megan Stern

Church was co-produced by the Vienna Festival 2008, the Wexner Center for the Arts at The Ohio State University and Performance Space 122. It was a National Performance Network Creation Fund project co-commissioned by Walker Art Center, in partnership with the Philadelphia Live Arts Festival and Philly Fringe, and the National Performance Network. It was developed through the Artist in Residence Program at Brooklyn Arts Exchange.

Church was remounted in January 2008 by the Public Theater in New York. It was co-produced by Young Jean Lee's Theater Company and Timothy Childs. It was performed at the Public with the same artistic team and the following cast:

REVEREND JOSÉ	Brian Bickerstaff
REVERED KATY	Katy Pyle
REVEREND WEENA	Weena Pauly
REVEREND KATIE	Katie Workum
CHOIR DIRECTOR	Stephanie Pistello
SOLOIST	Megan Stern

Characters

REVEREND JOSÉ
REVEREND KARINNE
REVEREND WEENA
REVEREND KATIE
SIXTY-PERSON CHOIR
CHOIR DIRECTOR
SOLOIST

Note on Performance

The performers are natural and sincere at all times. They should come across as real Christians who are doing an actual church service. They are unpretentious and appealing and never seem fake, pushy or creepy. The performers address the entire audience, looking around from face to face and not letting anyone escape what they're saying. Reverend José in particular likes to hold the audience captive, pacing around and sometimes singling people out and pointing at them as he speaks. Everyone speaks with total conviction—we believe that they believe what they're saying, no matter how bizarre their language becomes. The four reverends are good friends and acknowledge each other in supportive ways whenever possible (for example, when they pass each other during transitions). The female reverends should be named after whoever is playing them, but Reverend José (who was not Latino in the original production) is always Reverend José.

The audience enters the theater in silence. There is a simple wooden pulpit downstage center and two plain wood benches upstage on either side of the pulpit.

"Sherburne," performed by the Alabama Sacred Harp Singers from the album Songs of Christmas from the Alan Lomax Collection, *begins as the lights abruptly cut out.*

The song continues to play in the darkness. The singers' voices seem to come from everywhere, overwhelming the audience with their raw power.

The song ends.

In the dark, from behind the audience, Reverend José begins speaking.

REVEREND JOSÉ: Once upon a time, there was a young man who worried about a great many things.

He worried about money. He worried about having too much to do and not enough time. He worried about his health. He worried about his future. He worried about saying the wrong thing. He worried about being a hypocrite.

He woke up in the morning and his brain swam around in a fishbowl of worry until he fell asleep at night.

And the Lord said to him, "My child, open your eyes! Your world is as small as a speck of sand."

And the young man replied, "I am complicated. I am deep. I am a good person. I am sufficient."

(Pause.)

This is you.

You may not think this is you, but in fact you are incredibly similar to all the people sitting around you right now. The vast majority of them are doomed to a life of disappointing mediocrity just like yours.

And everyone sees how you yearn fruitlessly for glory when it is clearly already too late, and they pity you. They pity you as a grasping failure who pants for degrading miserable straws that are out of your reach.

And for those of you who have achieved some measure of pitiful worldly success, you look like fools! People laugh at you behind your back for the self-important way you speak, your pretensions, the way you ingratiate yourselves with the powerful. You are a buffoon who pretends that you don't care what anyone thinks of you, when in fact you writhe in ecstasy like a fondled dog each time a sycophantic halfwit praises your name.

Moreover, your popularity is already beginning to decline. You keep trotting out the same tricks again and again and you know deep in your heart that much of what you are doing is worthless trash, but you desperately cobble it together and present it to your clientele and some of them say, "Hey, I like this!" which enables you to limp pridefully towards your next pointless endeavor.

And let me not forget the most vainglorious among you: the quitters—who expected success without struggle and so quit to avoid disappointment.

All of you, you failures and successes and quitters, are deluded babies who believe that the world has yet to recognize your true greatness, when in fact you are a hanging piece of meat deteriorating towards sickness and death!

This is sin! This is sin, I tell you! You are sinning RIGHT NOW!

You sit there like pigs, stuffed fat with self-interest and anxiety. Your squinting eyeballs can barely protrude! YOU ARE A SPIRITUAL BLACK HOLE! Your spiritual bankruptcy is reflected in your endlessly repeating conversations about your struggles to quit smoking, quit drinking, quit junk food, quit caffeine, quit unsatisfying jobs and relationships—and this is what you talk about when you are trying to be deep! You claim to care about suffering in the world and take luxurious pleasure in raging against the perpetrators of that suffering, but this masturbation-rage helps nothing and no one!

You who are overworked and stressed-out! You who are trapped on the hamster wheel! You who burn with jealousy and bitterness! You for whom the glories of your former years are beginning to flame out and die! You who use alcohol and drugs and nicotine to numb your anxiety! YOU WHO FEEL THAT YOU ARE TOO FAT!

Let go.

Let go of these superficial earthly ties and deliver yourself in humility to the Lord.

He will open your eyes to the vast world! He will melt away the selfish pigfat from your face until your eyes stand forth true and clear!

For all of you Pharisees out there, I preach to you knowing that you may not heed my word. You will continue in your sin of obsessing and complaining and spending too much money. But the day will come in which the Lord God Almighty comes in a shining blaze of glory, and the knowledge of your shallow heart will cause you to bite through your own tongue with grief.

("Joshua Fit the Battle of Jericho," performed by Mahalia Jackson from the album Sunday Morning Prayer Meeting with Mahalia Jackson, *plays as lights fade up on Reverend Karinne, Reverend Weena and Reverend Katie entering. They wear pretty dresses with full skirts. Reverend Karinne wears a yellow dress, Reverend Weena wears a pink dress and Reverend Katie wears a blue dress. Each dress is slightly different in style from the others.*

They walk through the audience, greeting audience members.

Reverend José enters from the back, where he delivered his opening monologue, and begins greeting the audience.

All four performers are genuinely warm and friendly. As the song winds down, they make their way onto the stage. Reverend Katie sits on the bench stage left, Reverend Weena and Reverend José sit stage right. Reverend Karinne is bent down, talking to some people in the front row.

The song ends.

Reverend Karinne stands.)

REVEREND KARINNE: Hi, I'm Reverend Karinne, and this is Reverend Weena and Reverend Katie and Reverend José.

We're all really excited to be in *(Name of city)*, and we'd like to thank *(Name of venue)* for inviting us here and for taking such good care of us.

Anyway, before we get going, I'd like to ask if anyone has a prayer request.

(It occurs to her that the audience might not know what a prayer request is.)

A prayer request is basically just a request that everyone here pray for some issue you're struggling with.

(If anyone has a prayer request, Reverend Karinne asks for their name and requests that the audience pray for whatever issue the person just described.

If nobody has a prayer request [and she should wait for a good long uncomfortable while], then Reverend Karinne smiles at the audience and says the following:)

It's okay if you don't have any—I just like to ask.

REVEREND WEENA: Karinne, I have one actually.

(Reverend Weena goes to the pulpit as Reverend Karinne sits with Reverend Katie.)

Hi, I'm Reverend Weena and I recently broke up with my boyfriend of four years. Last week I bought a book called *How to Break Your Addiction to a Person*, from which I learned that what makes me addicted to unsuitable partners is a memory from babyhood of being dependent for life upon my mother, and that the feeling I am going to die without my ex-boyfriend is an illusion. I'd like to request your prayers during this difficult time as I struggle to conquer my obsession with self-help and stop wasting time on these silly books.

(She sits back down while Reverend Katie goes to the pulpit.)

REVEREND KATIE: Hi, I'm Reverend Katie, and actually I have a prayer request. Ever since I took on the role of tour manager, I've been experiencing a lot of stress. I've been working sixteen-hour days for weeks on end, my e-mail inbox is constantly full, and I have to be on the phone all day long.

Please keep me in your prayers as I work through my issues with whining.

I would also like to send our prayers to Reverend Wong, Reverend Morales, Reverend Mfume and Reverend Running Deer, who can't be with us *("this afternoon"/ "tonight")* because they are pursuing mission work in the field.

Hebrews, Chapter 13:

Let brotherly love continue.
Be not forgetful to entertain strangers: for thereby
   some have entertained angels unawares.
Remember them that are in bonds, as bound with
   them; and them which suffer adversity, as being
   yourselves also in the body.
Let your conversation be without covetousness; and
   be content with such things as ye have: for he hath
   said, I will never leave thee, nor forsake thee.
So that we may boldly say, The Lord is my helper,
   and I will not fear what man shall do unto me.
By him therefore let us offer the sacrifice of praise
   to God continually, that is, the fruit of our lips
   giving thanks to his name.
But to do good and to communicate forget not: for
   with such sacrifices God is well pleased.
Pray for us: for we trust we have a good conscience,
   in all things willing to live honestly.
Grace be with you all. Amen.

(She sits back down as Reverend José goes to the pulpit.)

REVEREND JOSÉ: When I was growing up, my family went to an evangelical church in an abandoned furniture store. It was the kind of church where nobody dressed up and everyone sat on metal folding chairs. There wasn't even a piano, just an electronic keyboard played by the local photographer, and a song leader who led all the songs like this:

(He imitates the song leader, raising his hands in the air and waving them slowly from side to side, with his eyes closed and a repulsively ecstatic expression on his face.)

I vowed that I would turn my back on Christianity as soon as I left home, and I did.

I don't have one of those classic testimonial stories about how I degenerated into drug addiction and alcoholism and sexual depravity until I hit bottom and found the Lord. Did I drink? Yes. Did I engage in the occasional use of recreational drugs? Yes. Did I sometimes go to work with a hangover? Yes. But nothing very terrible ever happened to me and I generally had a good time.

You see, I know you. Most of you are doing pretty well. There are quite a few non-Christians out there tonight who are feeling all right, who are surrounded by love and friendship and conduct fulfilling lives.

(Pointing at someone) You are busy all the time with work and family and projects and social engagements.

(Pointing at someone else) You wake up in the morning and answer e-mails and go to meetings and earn your living and frequently you are stressed-out, you get overwhelmed, but at night you relax and enjoy yourself and before you know it, it's morning again. The days pass by so quickly you barely notice their passing, and you go on like this for a long time, and it is good.

This is what I call the machine—the blissful robotic machine-like state of life that is the highest state of happiness a human being can attain.

You may be sitting out there today very happy.

(Pointing at someone) You may be in a wonderful relationship, *(Pointing at someone else)* love your children, *(Pointing at someone else)* enjoy your work and find it fulfilling, *(Pointing at someone else)* have caring friends. But any of these things could be taken away at any moment.

(Pointing at someone) Your perfect health is wiped out when you find out that you have cancer.

(Pointing at someone else) Or a car accident snaps your spine and takes the use of your legs.

(Pointing at someone else) Your partner is killed and leaves you alone.

(Pointing at someone else) Or else betrays you and leaves you for another relationship.

(Pointing at someone else) Your children are kidnapped and violated and tortured.

(Pointing at someone else) You are no longer able to work at the same pace and level as you used to.

(Pointing at someone else) You age, you grow older.

(Pointing at someone else) You lose your looks.

Your mind weakens, your body fails, and you begin to long for death. But it's not just the flesh that fails. Sometimes you get depressed, you feel like you can't do anything so you lie around like a slug, saying negative things and making the people who love you miserable.

And then there are those of you for whom this depression is your regular state, and any other feeling is an anomaly. You are the ones who lack healthy romantic relationships, or close friends, or a fulfilling career, or any kind of success in life. The mindless work of your days gives way to solitary nights and weekends, and the daily pleasures others take for granted are for you rare treats to be looked forward to and remembered.

I'd also like to acknowledge those of you who have been struck by heartbreak and loss and had a hard time even making it out here *("this afternoon"/"tonight")*, and to all of you I say that God can help you.

I'm not going to stand up here and tell you that God exists. I don't know that God exists any more than I know that God doesn't exist. The truth is that the world is a mystery. But I am telling you that I believe in God with an absolute certainty that comes from faith, and he is everything to me.

And I keep referring to God as a "he" because this is a patriarchal, sexist culture and many people find it more comforting to think of God as a father—but you can call God whatever you want.

We are a culture obsessed with willpower. We believe that with enough determination and positive thinking, we can control our futures. But as anyone who has ever lived through real tragedy knows, our world is a cruel and senseless one, and without God we are completely at its mercy.

God is love, and humans are filled with sin.

(Pointing at someone) Every single day, you deny happiness to the people you love by insisting on your need to be right, *(Pointing at someone else)* your need to do things your way, *(Pointing at someone else)* your need to have everything go the way you want it to.

Why is it so impossible for us to sacrifice our comfort to ease the suffering of another?

The reason is that for us, the fight between good and evil is a spectator sport. All you have to do to be a hero is root for the right side. If injustice makes you angry and suffering makes you sad, then you can be a good person without ever having to leave your couch.

And Jesus didn't go around picking on people for having premarital sex or drinking too much or being homosexuals—he wasn't interested in condemning people for their personal lives. Jesus was interested in the things that *we* experience as clichéd abstractions: police brutality, illegal immigrants in prison, the child living in poverty trying to do his homework without electricity.

Instead of fighting evil, we are consumed by it. All of the greatest evil that has ever been done in the world has been done by people who are prospering and terrified, just like you.

And I know that you may not heed my word. I know
that you will leave this service and go to a bar or restaurant or your comfortable home and consume food and
drink and indulge yourself and keep worrying about
petty things because this is all you've ever known, and to
tear oneself from the thing one has always known is very
difficult.

But I want to tell you that there is a door.

I know you are caged right now and that escape feels
impossible, but there is a shining door that is waiting for
you, and that door leads to God.

You don't need me to tell you what to do. You already
know what to do, you have always known it.

You just don't want to do it.

*(Reverend José returns to his seat. Reverend Weena goes to
the pulpit.)*

REVEREND WEENA: We believe that all of Jesus's political
beliefs are right and just and that we must stand against
racial discrimination, homophobia, anti-abortion, capi-
tal punishment, commercialism, war and indifference.

REVEREND JOSÉ, REVEREND KARINNE AND REVEREND
KATIE: God is life.

REVEREND WEENA: We believe that it is sin to engage in
masturbation-rage against the perpetrators of this evil
without doing anything concrete to create change. We
believe that pontificating and making art about political
subjects doesn't count as concrete action and is a form of
masturbation-rage.

REVEREND JOSÉ, REVEREND KARINNE AND REVEREND
KATIE: Jesus Christ is Lord.

REVEREND WEENA: We believe that the attempt to become a
better person through healthy living and therapy and
self-help is as wrongful as living a polluted and dys-
functional lifestyle if one is only focused on the self.

REVEREND JOSÉ, REVEREND KARINNE AND REVEREND
KATIE: The Spirit is love.
REVEREND KARINNE: Dear God Lord please have mercy on me.
REVEREND WEENA: This is my testimony. Once upon a time
I was bad and did drugs in every color of the rainbow.
Blue and purple and brown and gold, and I took them all
at once and washed them down with whiskey. And I was
in my bathrobe, and then I smoked some pot.

Then I found some prostitutes and did sin with them,
and then I found some pipes and banged the prostitutes
on the head, and it was good. And then I wandered
through the gutter where there were some chickens lying
around and I stuck the pipes right through them so that
the blood gushed upwards like a fountain, and I stuck my
mouth over the pipe and let the blood gush upwards into
my mouth and lift me up into the sky. And I was raised
about ten feet into the air by this gushing tower of chicken
blood, and I didn't care. I was floating and free.

And then everything went black and I woke up in a
hotel room with a swastika on my forehead, naked with
one leg shaved. And I didn't care. I got up and put on
some clothes and walked out, and there happened upon
a friend of mine, drunk, stumbling, with only one shoe
and carrying one of those net bags filled with oranges.

And this was life. We would trespass onto military
bases, climbing over the barbed wire and running
around, and have sex with multiple partners in multiple
configurations. And there were many unwanted preg-
nancies lined up in jars on our bureau tables, which we
would count as trophies in our war on conventionality.

And we were really happy. Oh boy were we happy. We
enjoyed ourselves thoroughly. And then one day I heard
a voice in the darkness of my hangover, calling through
my deathlike sleep, and I sat up and asked, "Yes, Lord?"
and I don't know why I said that but I did, and I ripped
off my sleep-mask to find Satan sitting on my chest.

It was the heaviest weight I had ever felt in my life. And I asked, "Satan, why do you sit upon my chest in the nighttime?" And Satan said, "I sit upon your chest in the nighttime because you are blind and do not see your own misery, and I like that. I like that you are so messed up. It makes me feel good. And I would just like to sit here and enjoy you for a moment."

And I was sore afraid. And I learned nothing from this, nor felt any more, for the next ten years. Now, with the fellowship of my friends, I have learned from this lesson. I have learned that none of that stuff mattered at all, and that sin has nothing to do with being messed up. Amen.

(Reverend Weena exits with Reverend Karinne and Reverend Katie following her.

Reverend José sits by himself on the bench.

He slowly rises, goes to the pulpit, and stands looking at the audience.

In the following sermon, Reverend José is more passionate and dramatic than he was in his previous sermon, but he preaches with total conviction and is never cartoonish or silly.)

REVEREND JOSÉ *(Violently thrusting both arms in the air and shouting toward the ceiling)*: Dear Heavenly Father, I invoke thee! I invoke thee to come down here in a circle of blazing fire and show us your face! I invoke thee to unlock the cage door of our self-absorption and bless us in your love forever and ever amen!

(He looks at the audience, normal tone.)

Hello. My name is José and I am a preacher. I live on the mountainside. I go to the mountainside and there is a goat that kisses me and I am its best friend. The love of Jesus is a little baby goat that comes to you and kisses

18

you and eats sand out of your hand. And the reason why I give it sand is that sand is warm and golden and kissed by the sun. And little baby goats like to eat things like tin cans.

And what I want to tell you about Jesus today is that Jesus did not have a beard, nor wear sandals. Jesus was a fiery star shot out of the firmasphere straight from the molten heart of the Lord God Almighty.

And that shining baby star grew up to be a man, a great man who walked among the lepers and kissed their scabs, who held hands with the diseased child molesters and never shrank away in disgust. And he had five favorite child molesters who were all reformed, and they bowed down before him and offered him oil and wine. And he partook of it even though all of the Pharisees shrank back and were disgusted.

Do you know what the word "grandeur" means?

It means almightiness.

(Pointing at someone) And I can see that *you* have an almightiness in *your soul* that is far greater than any of your paltry ambitions.

It is more majestic than a cave buried in the darkest jungle, with rivers of molten pearl trickling through boulder-sized diamonds, and emerald ferns springing through cracks in sapphire walls. And a grand spiral staircase that swings out to reveal a hidden room of magical treasures and swords, while the world's sweetest honey drips from ruby chandeliers and envelops everything before solidifying into purest amber and rolling into the corners. And ripe peaches bursting with fragrance sagging from ornamental trees decorated with old roots and beets.

The glory in your soul is more splendid than all of these pitiful things.

Now I want to tell you a parable.

Once upon a time there was a lamp seller who also sold sandals. His lamps were more popular than his sandals, but his heart was invested in the sandals because they were more artistic. One day the Lord came to him and said, "I would like one lamp." And the lamp seller said, "Why does everyone just want lamps? Why doesn't anyone want to buy my beautiful sandals?" And Jesus said, "I want to tell you the parable of the tuna and the bird. One day, the tuna said to the bird, 'Why do you always fly in the sky and never swim in the sea with me?' And the bird said, 'Because flying in the sky is superior and going below the water is beneath me.' And the fish said, 'If going below the water is beneath you, then what happens when you go beneath the tree?'"

(He looks at the audience meaningfully.)

Now the message of that story is that you should never think you are better than anyone else, including yourself.

Another thing I want to talk about today is mummies. Mummies is the curse of the devil. As you all know from movies and television, mummies eat cotton balls and excrete them on the sidewalk to serve as an affliction to all who walk there.

And I want to tell you that you are a little baby still in your mind. You are a little baby lying there helpless and weak and without reason in your swaddling clothes, vulnerable to all danger. And you cling to your alcohol and your drugs and your caffeine like a baby pacifier, but in reality you are all mummies and not babies at all. You are grown, adult mummies and you live in a mummy cave.

And another thing I forgot to tell you is that Satan is a mummy. Mummies are real because they are Satan's minions. They are independent and free and they can live just as well without you as with you, because we have the modern technology today that enables mummies to drink human blood that is infected with the AIDS virus, and yet the mummies are not harmed because they are magical creatures.

And I know that some of you may not believe in magic.

You may think, "These stories from the Bible are all about unbelievable magic and I don't believe it." But the truth is that *you* are magic.

(Pointing at someone) The blood pumping through *your* veins, *(Pointing at someone)* the thoughts pumping through *your* head, are all magic, and even the most brilliant scientists agree that most things about us are a mystery.

You must look into the poisons of your life and recognize them as what they are: poison. You must look at that cup of coffee that the waitress puts in front of you at the diner and think, "Don't drink that. It's poison!" When you are bouncing the fruit of your loins upon your knee, experiencing ego-glory as you gaze upon your own likeness, you must warn yourself, "Poison!" And when you are out at a restaurant laughing and talking with your friends while spending twenty-dollar bills on cocktails and appetizers, you must heed the call, "Poison!"

And when that romantic interest in your life appears, eager to bestow upon you whatever scrap of time or energy or attention is left when they tire of running on the hamster wheel of their self-centered lives, you must look upon that person as a pillar of poison that will turn you to freezing stone if you touch it.

I have walked through the wilderness, and I have seen the cacti looming, bulbous as watermelons, their long quills extruding like hairs from a boil. And then their bobbing forms were upon me, piercing my heart like a grape and lifting me high into the air whilst my blood pooled at their feet.

And then the Devil tempted me, "Would you like me to lift you from that cactus?" And I said, "NO! GET THEE BACK, SATAN because I am a child of the Lord and this is the Lord's testing unto me and I will never turn forth my face unto your evildoing!"

And then the Devil ran away in tears, because he was also once the Lord's child and still felt the pang of that loss.

And then one day as I was walking down an icy street I saw a beautiful pathway of stars stretched out before me leading up to the sky, and a unicorn came to me and said, "My dear son, I am coming to you in this vision because I knew that you would accept me in no other way. You are in the grips of a powerful fetishistic obsession with magic and fantasy, which are of the Devil, and you can see nothing that is not filtered through that evil. I am here to tell you that I am a mummy, an evil mummy who wants to turn you away from the Lord and lure you into the valley of suffering and death.

"I want to squeeze your heart in my fist until all the blood drains into my grasping, suckling mouth! I want to empoison the crevices of your brain until it shrivels up like a slug beneath the salt!"

And I woke up in the hospital shaking, for I had been sucked into a combine. I was going to die just like my father before me.

And as I saw my mother's face wet with tears and struggled for my last breath, I realized that greatness resides only in God.

(Reverend José exits. Reverend Karinne enters and goes to pulpit.)

REVEREND KARINNE: There was a complicated situation with my Lord and this little set of miniature Nativity dolls and furniture I had. And some evil demons who really scared me but finally I told my Lord all about it when I thought it was all over. But then I was rearranging the little Mary and Joseph, trying to figure out how to trick everyone and escape, but oh before that this blond seductress was trying to tempt me but she kept making these disgusted faces and I asked her why are you doing this and she said there was a camera filming it as evidence against me and somehow I managed to escape. At one point I desperately grabbed at a doorknob and it was open and I managed to escape knowing my mind could bend reality and using my will to make it happen. And then back at my parents' old house I moved the Nativity set and a scary man noticed they were moved and I made up some lie but he knew and I knew I would be tortured forever, and he cornered me in the bathroom and I shoved my fingers down his throat as far as they would go and he started spewing out everything inside him, but it was represented as objects and not vomit. The vomiting was represented by men at a garbage dump throwing stuff in the air and I escaped and it was winter and stood at the bus terminal waiting in line, but the lady said the bus was canceled so I was walking in the snow and then a huge fight with villains maybe with the floating superhuman good angel helping, and I was about to jump into this luxury car (I was on a bus before and the bus driver girl said she had friends coming with some kind of SUV) and my old revolutionary friend with a machine gun took me to a war-torn-looking courtyard to eat bento boxes with tempura, and he said everyone was really happy there. And it ended with a fight in a big room. The evil demon had been captured, blinded, and his hands tied together, but he got his hands free and just started punching people out left and right blindly and I jumped on a table and ran. And a floating superhuman good angel and a floating superhuman bad angel and I were fighting to the death, but I don't remember which one I was.

(Reverend Karinne looks at the audience with sad eyes.
She takes a microphone from behind the pulpit and begins to sing an a cappella version of "Bread" by on!air!library!, from the album on!air!library! *She sings*

sweetly and earnestly. Reverend Katie and Reverend Weena enter with microphones and sing the harmony.)

REVEREND KARINNE:
The reason why you don't rest
The reason why you don't see . . .
Layer by
Layer you lay
Layer by
Layer you lay *conela*

REVEREND KATIE AND
REVEREND WEENA:

The reason why you don't rest	Shakin' in your bones is required
	To dream up large colossal empires
You haven't built it	
The reason why you don't see	Shakin' in your bones is required
The reason why you don't rest	Shakin' in your bones is required
	To dream up large colossal empires
You haven't built it	
The reason why you don't see	Shakin in your bones is required
Layer by	Shakin' in your
Layer you lay	Bones
A brick for me	
Layer by	Shakin' in your
Layer you lay	Bones
Layer by	Layer by
Layer you lay	Layer you lay
A brick for me	
Layer by	Layer by
Layer you lay	Layer you lay

24

Shakin' in your bones is
    required
To dream up large
    colossal empires
Shakin' in your bones is
    required
Shakin' in your bones is
    required
To dream up large
    colossal empires
Shakin in your bones is
    required

Oo oo oo *(Hums first
    verse melody)*

The reason why you don't
    rest
The reason why you don't
    see
Layer by
Layer you lay
A brick for me
Layer by
Layer you lay.

Shakin' in your bones is
    required
To dream up large
    colossal empires
Shakin' in your bones is
    required
Shakin' in your bones is
    required
To dream up large
    colossal empires
Shakin in your bones is
    required

Oo oo oo oo *(Hum harmony)*

Oo oo oo oo

Oo oo oo oo

Oo oo
Oo oo

Oo oo
Oo oo.

(The song ends.
    The reverends bow their heads.
    Reverend Katie prays, quietly and with emotion.)

REVEREND KATIE: Dear Lord, thank you for my family.
    Thank you for the fact that they are safe and well and not
    in danger of being driven from their homes or blown up
    in the street. I am grateful that I have a place to sleep and
    enough to eat and that I have friends who care about me.
    Thank you for cold water and hot water and heaters and

air-conditioning and blankets and reading in bed. Thank you for my education. I appreciate being able to do what I want with my life, to choose how to make myself useful in the world. I appreciate my health, my sight, my hearing, and my limbs. I am grateful that I can make a living in a way that is neither dangerous nor inhumane. Thank you, dear Heavenly Father, for these gifts. I know that no matter what happens, your love and power will never forsake me and I will be comforted and at peace. Please help me to love you and others more than I love feeding my ego and pride, and make your love manifest in mine so that others can see your glory. And for all these people who came out to *(Name of venue, "this afternoon"/ "tonight")*, whatever they may be feeling or thinking right now, please bless them in everything they do and watch over them as they make their way home. Amen.

("Every Move I Make," performed by Passion from the album I Could Sing of Your Love Forever, *begins.*

Reverend José moves the pulpit off to the side and remains there to watch the female reverends.

The female reverends remove their shoes and put them under the benches.

They do a long, exuberant dance number with lots of turns, kicks, jumps, spins and leaps. Just when you think the dance is going to end, it morphs into something new. It's an endless, challenging, exhausting dance, but the female reverends are filled with the spirit and radiate joy through each new movement.

Finally, the female reverends break off into ecstatic solo dances. Reverend Katie runs to Reverend José and pulls him into the dance. They all jam out together.

Reverend José takes off his jacket and hurls it to the floor.

The female reverends resume their choreographed dance. Then Reverend José suddenly falls in with them, in sync with the end of the dance.

The song ends.
The female reverends exit.
Reverend José stands alone. He goes to the jacket he threw on the floor, picks it up, dusts it off, and lays it carefully over the stage right bench.)

REVEREND JOSÉ: Once upon a time, there was a young man. He grew up in a wealthy family and was a weakling ineffectual boy the whole time he was growing up. He had an older brother who was good at sports and always had girlfriends, but the weakling never had any girlfriends. He never had *any* friends. This weakling never had any success or fun in life, until he discovered pornography.

When he became an adult, he had dandruff and body odor, and he always lived with his mother. When his mother moved into a nursing home, he moved in too. But one day his older brother came and took his mother away, and the weakling retaliated by suing him. The nursing home tried to get the weakling to leave as well, but he wouldn't budge, and he threatened them with lawyers until eventually they gave up.

And at this nursing home was a young woman, working for minimum wage. She had diabetes and chronic back pain and had been supporting herself since she was fifteen years old. She had lived alone for years and knew what that was.

And she was as popular at the nursing home as the weakling was despised. She was smart and funny and was always saying ridiculous things to make the old people laugh.

While everyone else shunned the weakling, the young woman asked him about his likes and dislikes, and occasionally slid record albums under his door. In the beginning, the weakling was rude and ungrateful, but every night, she prayed for him. And as she spent more time with him, he began to open up, describing humiliations from his childhood, his desire to find his mother, and his love of boats. And he listened sympathetically to her as she talked about her health problems, her dream of having a garden, and her hopes of finding a boyfriend, and they developed a friendship that was valuable to both.

One day, the weakling's older brother came to the nursing home to end the lawsuit and make peace with him, and the weakling was sore afraid. As he sat in the lounge area awaiting his brother, who was late, he could feel himself trembling. The young woman, knowing his fears, sat nearby speaking encouraging words, which he accepted gratefully. When his brother appeared, tall and striking in a handsome suit, the weakling stood up with as much confidence as he could and shook his brother's hand, saying, "Good to see you, Desmond," and the young woman slipped away. As the two men talked over their legal affairs, they both felt awkward, but the older brother was mild and reasonable and the weakling finally agreed to withdraw his lawsuit. At the conclusion of the meeting, the young woman appeared with the older brother's coat and the weakling said, "This is Joanne. She's been working here for almost six years." His brother said, "Nice to meet you, Joanne." The weakling said, "She may not be the most attractive girl in the world and her education is less than negligible, but she works damned hard, which is more than I can say for the rest of these people." The weakling's brother collected his coat, thanked Joanne, and disappeared from the weakling's life forever.

From that day forward, the weakling never spoke another kind word to his young friend. He made belittling remarks to her face and insulted her before others. And when he was thrown in jail for keying the car of a man who angered him, she bailed him out. When he had a stroke and lay in a hospital bed, she read to him about boats.

And every night, Joanne would go home to her dingy apartment and take off her shoes and cook her meal and hope that she could fall asleep. And one night, she lay down and found herself on a light-filled plain surrounded by trees made of water and fish made of birds and all manner of unimaginable-looking things. And everything kept changing shape—mountains turning to fruit turning to wind turning to things she couldn't identify—and she kept changing shape as well. A serpent appeared, asking why she didn't stand up for herself and have more fun in life, and then metamorphosed into a pile of onions that tumbled to her feet before drifting off one by one in the form of rabbits that became thunder that became oceans.

And finally, over a hill, she saw all the Faithful—the Faithful who had loved and struggled and suffered—coming towards her, overjoyed that she had joined them at last. And suddenly, Jesus himself was there, and the delight she knew thereafter is not ours to comprehend until death.

Hallelujah.

(A woman enters the house singing the spiritual "Ain't Got Time to Die." She is followed by a diverse, sixty-person choir that enters singing in single file. The effect should be akin to that of clowns emerging endlessly from a clown car.

Finally they are all onstage, led by an enthusiastic choir director dressed in black who shakes her booty and does silly things to make the choir laugh. The choir is a motley-looking crew, unified only by their white shirts and black bottoms [which are different in style—some people wear black jeans, some wear dress clothes], but they sing ecstatically and with total religious conviction.

The song is a call-and-response between the soloist, who has a massive voice, and the choir. At the climax of the song, the entire choir begins clapping and dancing with joyous abandon.

The song ends.)

END OF PLAY

Songs of the Dragons
Flying to Heaven

For Stephen Booth

Production History

Songs of the Dragons Flying to Heaven was originally produced by Young Jean Lee's Theater Company. It premiered
in September 2006 at HERE Arts Center in New York through
HERE'S HARP residency program. It was directed by Young
Jean Lee; the set and lighting design were by Eric Dyer, the
costume design was by Colleen Werthmann, the sound
design was by Jamie McElhinney and the video and choreography were by Dean Moss. It was performed by:

KOREAN-AMERICAN	Becky Yamamoto
KOREAN 1	Jun Sky Kim
KOREAN 2	Haerry Kim
KOREAN 3	Jennifer Lim
WHITE PERSON 1	Juliana Francis Kelly
WHITE PERSON 2	Brian Bickerstaff

Characters

KOREAN-AMERICAN
KOREAN 1
KOREAN 2
KOREAN 3
WHITE PERSON 1
WHITE PERSON 2

Note

Korean-American and Koreans 1, 2 and 3 should be played
by actresses who are one hundred percent Korean, Chinese
or Japanese (or any mix of the three, for example, half-
Chinese/half-Japanese). When speaking English, Koreans 1,
2 and 3 speak with authentic Asian accents and Korean-
American speaks with an American accent. When not speaking English, Koreans 1, 2 and 3 speak their native languages,
whatever those may be. Ideally, one would speak Korean, one
would speak Chinese and one would speak Japanese. In the
original production, Koreans 1 and 2 spoke Korean and
Korean 3 spoke Cantonese, which is reflected in the stage
directions.

White Person 1 is female and White Person 2 is male.

The audience enters the theater and finds itself stuck behind the set, which is a quasi-Korean-Buddhist temple with a large, multipaneled Korean dragon mural painted on the back. There are rafters extending above the walls, suggesting the elements of an Asian-looking roof. Colored paper lanterns hang from the ceiling to the rear and sides of the temple, and there is the sound of Asian flute music and trickling water. Ushers prevent people from going around the sides of the temple in order to reach their seats. Ideally, the audience will be crowded together behind the temple in a claustrophobic manner and made to steep in this oppressively "Asian" environment for a long time before they are allowed to go to their seats.

As soon as the house opens, the sound stops and the audience enters down narrow gravel paths on either side of the temple. The inside of the temple is a large, bare room made of sheets of unpainted light birch plywood. There are two actor entrances, one on each side of the room. The stage floor is also made from unpainted light birch plywood, except for a large rectangle in the center, which is made from knotty yellow pine planks, approximating the pattern of floor planking in many Korean Buddhist temples. The entire floor is raised slightly and does not meet the walls, giving it a floating quality. The overall effect is one of emptiness and light.

There are four evenly spaced rows of one-inch diameter fluorescent tubes running upstage to downstage suspended over the set, suggesting a ceiling for the temple. Only the tubes themselves are visible—no housing or wiring. The two stage left rows of lights extend over the audience to serve as house lighting. Each of the White People's scenes are lit by the tubes directly above where they are standing (which changes with each scene), except for the final scene, during which all of the tubes are lit at once.

Sudden lights out.

Prerecorded sound of the play's writer and director Young Jean Lee and her real-life friends talking and laughing as they begin to make a video of Young Jean getting hit in the face. Dean is operating the camera and Yehuda is hitting Young Jean. Rollo is helping with the lighting. The entire dialogue plays in darkness and the audience can't see anything that is taking place.

DEAN: Okay . . . Everybody ready?

YEHUDA: So do a, just do a practice for the camera.

DEAN: That's it.

YEHUDA: All right. So.

DEAN: Hold on. Just . . .

YEHUDA: On a scale of one to ten what should this be?

YOUNG JEAN: Mmm . . .

YEHUDA: Ten being as hard as I'm going to hit you, not as hard as I can hit you.

YOUNG JEAN: Right. Um, you know, I think we should be in, like, communication for the whole thing, because when we did it, it was fine when there was talking. So why don't you start out, like, pretty soft, and then, you know, like start out with like a one, and then I'll tell you to, like, increase it.

(Everyone giggles as Yehuda lightly taps Young Jean's face.)

36

ROLLO: A caress.

YOUNG JEAN: Are we rolling?

DEAN: We are rolling. Okay . . . go.

(Slap.)

YOUNG JEAN *(Giggling)*: That's pretty hard, for a one. Like, projecting to a ten.

DEAN: Yehuda, when you slap her, don't stop. Follow through. Follow through so the hand disappears and we only have her reaction.

YEHUDA: I'll go softer, all right?

YOUNG JEAN: No, you can try it that—like that again.

YEHUDA: Ready?

(Slap.)

YOUNG JEAN: Dean, is this okay?

DEAN: One more time. This is okay. Um, Young Jean, I have a sense that you want to . . . come back.

YOUNG JEAN: Come back where?

DEAN: Come back to the front, and come back to your composure as quickly as possible.

YOUNG JEAN: As quickly as possible?

DEAN: As quickly as you possibly can.

YOUNG JEAN: Okay.

DEAN: I know you're, you're kind of figuring out a lot of information.

YOUNG JEAN: Yeah.

DEAN: But try to—

YOUNG JEAN: Try to just come back—

DEAN: Try to, try to come back and let that be the figuring out.

YEHUDA: Yeah, that should be your blocking, because even if you can't do that, it'll look cool.

DEAN: Okay. Long neck. Thank you.

(Slap.)

Good.

(Slap.)

Better. Yehuda, that was better.
YEHUDA: Okay.

(Slap.)

DEAN: Young Jean, fix your hair.

(Slap.)

Chin up. Debutante.

(Really loud slap.)

Yehuda, not any harder than that.

(Slap.)

Hair. Beautiful.

> *(Slap.*
> *Pause.*
> *Slap.*
> *Pause.*
> *Slap.*
> *Young Jean sniffles.*
> *Slap.)*

You can't be the signal.
YOUNG JEAN: Hm?
DEAN: You can't be the signal.

YEHUDA: I'm just saying it—you don't have to answer, I'm just gonna say it.
YOUNG JEAN: Okay.

(Slap.
A siren in the background.)

DEAN: Hair.

(Slap.
Young Jean sniffles.
Slap.
Young Jean sniffles.
Slap.)

Okay let's stop.
YOUNG JEAN *(Sniffling)*: Why?
DEAN: Okay let's not.

(A video of Young Jean crying appears against the back wall. A traditional Korean pansori song begins. Young Jean gets hit in the face repeatedly. The video is edited so that you never see the hand hitting her face—only her reaction as her head flies back and she tries to straighten her hair and regain her composure. She cries throughout.
The slaps increase in intensity and frequency, continuing after the song ends, until you see Young Jean mouth the words, "One more," before she gets hit one last time.
The video ends.
Lights come up on Korean-American, looking cute in a T-shirt, jeans and sneakers.
She smiles at the audience.)

KOREAN-AMERICAN: Have you ever noticed how most Asian-Americans are slightly brain-damaged from having grown up with Asian parents?

It's like being raised by monkeys—these retarded monkeys who can barely speak English and who are too evil to understand anything besides conformity and status. Most of us hate these monkeys from an early age and try to learn how to be human from school or television, but the result is always tainted by this subtle or not so subtle retardation. Asian people from Asia are even more brain-damaged, but in a different way, because they are the original monkey.

Anyway, some white men who like Asian women seem to like this retarded quality as well, and sometimes the more retarded the better.

I am so mad about all of the racist things against me in this country, which is America.

Like the fact that the reason why so many white men date Asian women is that they can get better-looking Asian women than they can get white women because we are easier to get and have lower self-esteem. It's like going with an inferior brand so that you can afford more luxury features. Also, Asian women will date white guys who no white woman would touch.

But the important thing about being Korean is getting to know your roots. Because we come to this country and want to forget about our ancestry, but this is bad, and we have to remember that our grandfathers and grandmothers were people too, with interesting stories to tell.

Which leads to a story from my grandmother, which is the story of the mudfish.

In Korea they have this weird thing where everyone turns a year older on New Year's Day. So if you were born on December 31st, you turn one on January 1st even though you've only been alive for a day. Anyway, each year on New Year's Day, my grandmother used to make this special dish called meekudaji tong that she would only serve once a year because it was such a pain in the ass to make.

The main ingredient of meekudaji tong is mudfish, which are these tiny fishes they have in Korea that live on muddy riverbanks and eat mud. Every New Year's Day, my grandmother would throw a bunch of mudfish into a bowl of brine, which would make them puke out all their mud until they were shiny clean. Then she would put pieces of tofu on a skillet, heat it up, and throw the live mudfish onto the skillet. The mudfish would frantically burrow inside the pieces of tofu to escape the heat and, voilà, stuffed tofu!

White people are so alert to any infringement on their rights. It's really funny. And the reason why it's funny is that minorities have all the power. We can take the word racism and hurl it at people and demolish them, and there's nothing you can do to stop us.

I feel so much pity for you right now.

You have no idea what's going on. The wiliness of the Korean is beyond anything you could ever hope to imagine.

I can promise you one thing, which is that we will crush you.

You may laugh now, but remember my words when you and your offspring are writhing under our yoke.

(Raising her fist) Let the Korean dancing begin!

("I Was Born [A Unicorn]," performed by The Unicorns from the album Who Will Cut Our Hair When We're Gone?, *begins.)*

KOREAN 1 *(Offstage, in Korean)*: It's fun!
KOREAN 3 *(Offstage, in Cantonese)*: Yes, it's fun!

(Koreans 1, 2 and 3 run in from stage right, wearing brightly colored traditional Korean dresses. They shake the outer layer of their skirts above their heads so that they look like big balls of color, and run in manic circles

around Korean-American, who tries to smile but is weirded-out.

The Koreans lower their skirts and begin skipping in circles around Korean-American, swinging their skirts from side to side and getting closer and closer to her until their skirts are assaulting her face. The Koreans scatter and begin slapping each other playfully on the ass and giggling while Korean-American edges uneasily out of the way.

Korean 1 smacks Korean-American viciously on the ass. Korean 2 smacks Korean-American viciously on the ass. Korean-American makes, "What the fuck?" gesture.

The Koreans lift their skirts daintily and run in a wide circle, each whacking Korean-American audibly on the head as they pass her, and then resume playfully slapping each other on the ass.

Korean-American finally retaliates and angrily smacks Korean 2 hard on the ass. Korean 2 grabs Korean-American's hair and yanks her forward so that Korean-American's head collides with her knee, then punches her in the face. Korean 3 punches Korean-American in the face. Korean-American swings at Korean 1 and misses. Korean 1 kicks Korean-American in the stomach, sending her backward into Korean 3, who shoves Korean-American toward Korean 2, who smacks Korean-American with the back of her hand. Korean 3 grabs Korean-American and bites her shoulder until Korean-American hurls her to the ground. Korean 1 runs at Korean-American, who hurls Korean 1 to the ground. Korean 2 grabs Korean-American's hair, pulling her over the prone Korean 1 and yanking her to the floor. Korean 3 holds Korean-American under her arms while Korean 2 kicks her in the crotch. Korean 1 punches Korean-American in the gut, and Korean 3 rolls her over and spits on her.

The Koreans leave Korean-American passed out on the floor. They begin straightening out their dresses and hair, talking and smiling among themselves. They notice Korean-American trying to drag herself offstage and Korean 1 grabs her by the hair and punches her in the face repeatedly. Koreans 2 and 3 begin smiling and making peace signs with their fingers, which they shake frantically, as though someone in the audience is trying to take their picture. Korean 1 joins them and the three of them step over Korean-American's prostrate body, smiling and making peace signs.

Split-second blackout and flash as they step over Korean-American.

When the lights come back up, Korean 2 and Korean 3 are on their knees with their hands held straight above their heads [a traditional punishment in Korean schools], while Korean 1 stands over them watchfully. Korean-American crawls offstage and sits at the stage left entrance, watching the Koreans.

Note: the Koreans address each other by constantly changing fake-Asian names, so there's no use trying to keep track. Also, until the point indicated, all of the dialogue in this scene is spoken in Korean, except for Korean 3's lines, which are spoken in Cantonese. [Korean-American speaks in English throughout.]

Korean 2 makes a disgruntled face and rubs one of her arms.)

KOREAN 1: Keep still, Hyak-Jong!

KOREAN 2: My arm hurts!

KOREAN 1: Keep them up!

KOREAN 2: Why?

KOREAN 1: Because that is my order.

(To Korean 3) You too, Hyong-Mong!

KOREAN 2: I don't want to do this anymore!

KOREAN 1: Shut up!

KOREAN 2 *(Getting up)*: I revolt!

(Grabbing Korean 3 and dragging her up) We revolt!

*(Standoff between Korean 2 and Korean 1.
Korean 1 loses.)*

KOREAN 1: Fine.
Let's eat those pigs' ears we bought!

(They squat down and mime gnawing on pigs' ears.)

Do you have sex?
KOREAN 2: What?!
KOREAN 3: Who has had sex?
KOREAN 2: None of us!

(Everyone stares wide-eyed at Korean 1.)

Have you had sex, Mook-Jong?
KOREAN 1: What's the big deal?
KOREAN 3: Oh no!
KOREAN 1: I don't care, I like having sex. I like having sex
for money.
KOREAN 2: For money! Mook-Jong, have you become a
prostitute?
KOREAN 1: It's fun!

*(Korean 1 slaps Korean 2 on the ass and runs away.
Korean 2 runs after her. Korean 3 is left alone.
A scary Ghost-Man's voice sounds from nowhere.)*

GHOST-MAN: Ding-Jong! Ding-Jong!
KOREAN 3 *(Terrified)*: Leave me alone. I can't hear you!
GHOST-MAN: Diiiiiiiing-Jong! Can you see me?
KOREAN 3: I can't hear anything!
(Calling to her friends) Mook-Jong! Wing-Bong!
GHOST-MAN: Ding-Jong! What shall we play today?
KOREAN 3: I can't hear you!
GHOST-MAN: Shall we play "Hookers and Johns"?

KOREAN 3: No! I don't want to play that. I'm not like Mook-Jong! Please, please go away!

(Silence. Ghost-Man's voice disappears.
Korean 3 smiles with relief, then gets a glazed, pos-sessed look on her face.)

(Singing spookily, in English:)

> When you cut her
> Do not cut her with a knife.
> Do not chop her with an ax.
> Do not saw her with a saw.

(Slowly rising.)

> One, two, one, two.
> Now you know what you must do.
> Do not cut her with a knife.
> This is how you take her life.

> Put some fishhooks in her hand.
> That is all you need.
> She will put them in her cunt
> And they will make her bleed.

(As she sings, Korean 1 and Korean 2 reenter.
They are appalled.)

KOREAN 1: What are you singing, Ding-Jong?
KOREAN 3 *(Snapping out of it)*: What?
KOREAN 2: Why were you singing that bad song?
KOREAN 3: It's just an old Korean song I learned from my grandmother.
KOREAN 1: Don't sing it anymore.

KOREAN 3: Okay.
Mook-Jong, do you really have sex for money?
KOREAN 1: I don't know. Do you want to see my panties?

(She flashes up her skirt, revealing red ruffled panties, and giggles.)

KOREAN 2: Mook-Jong, you are only thirteen years old! How can you be so bad?
KOREAN 1: It's fun!

(She giggles and slaps Korean 3 on the ass.
Korean 2 puts on imaginary Walkman headphones.)

KOREAN 2: Ya, ya! *(Translation: "Hey, hey!")* Come quickly!

(The other girls run to her.)

KOREAN 1: What is it, Hyan-So?
KOREAN 2: It's our favorite song, playing on my Walkman!

(She shares her headphones with the other girls and they listen together. Everyone bobs their heads in unison.
"Small Waiting," performed by Cool [The (ku:l)] from the album Love Is . . . Waiting, *begins.*
The Koreans do a beautiful traditional Korean dance to the music.
Korean-American walks onstage, unable to resist the charming dance. The Koreans flutter past her in a circle and Korean 3 takes Korean-American gently by the waist, bringing her into the dance. Korean 3 encourages Korean-American to join in the dance. Korean-American imitates their movements clumsily, beaming with happiness. Korean 3 critically eyes Korean-American's dancing and makes a disgusted face, shoving her away. Korean-American glares at the Koreans through the rest of their dance.

When the dance ends, Korean-American makes racist faces at the Koreans. She makes "Chinese eyes" at Korean 2, mimes eating rice at Korean 1, does a karate chop to the audience, and bows to Korean 3—all while making big buck teeth. The Koreans are offended.

The song ends.

Korean-American exits, cracking up.

Korean 3 rushes center stage and bows. She elaborately mimes everything she says in a tragic manner.)

KOREAN 3: I am a Korean schoolgirl. I come from the village of Inchon. We are very poor in my village. One time, my teacher came over and drank soju with my father. My father said, "How many daughters must I sacrifice before you will raise the dishonor that has fallen upon my house?" My teacher said, "You only must give one, and that is little So-So." Which is me. So my father shook hands with my teacher and then my teacher took me into a little room and took my virginity.

(Korean 3 falls to the ground and hikes up her dress, revealing white ruffled panties. Korean 1 and Korean 2 enter in a hyperactive spaz and begin fussing with Korean 3's clothes and hair.)

KOREAN 1: Come, So-So, or we will be late for the big party at the Dragon Festival!

KOREAN 3 *(Tragically)*: Just a minute, Chu-Chu, I am braiding sorrow blossoms into my hair.

(Koreans 1 and 2 writhe with impatience, unable to contain their excitement.)

KOREAN 2: Soon it will be time for the Festival of the Falling Flowers!

KOREAN 1: My father has made a big paper dragon that I will wear on my head at the festival!

(Koreans 1 and 2 run around pretending to be dragons.)

KOREAN 2: So-So, let us dance, for I feel full of joy for the falling flowers.

(Koreans 1 and 2 dance hyperactively.)

KOREAN 3 *(Crying)*: Oh, Chu-Chu, how can I dance when my heart is still loaded with the sadness that comes from my way that I was deflowered?

(Without the others noticing, Korean-American crawls onstage and stops behind Korean 3.
Koreans 1 and 2 yank Korean 3 back and forth between them, forcing her into an unwilling dance.)

KOREAN 2: Oh, So-So, you must put unkind thoughts to rest and come dance with me on this most festive of occasions!

(Korean-American's hand reaches out from beneath Korean 3's skirt and grabs her thigh.
Korean 3 screams.)

What is wrong, So-So?
KOREAN-AMERICAN: Blood and gore are running down Korean 3's leg!

(The Koreans scream.)

(Sticking her head out from under Korean 3's skirt) A monster emerges from Korean 3's skirt, covered in blood and slime!

(Korean 3 screams. Koreans 1 and 2 look perplexed.
Korean-American crawls out from between Korean 3's
legs and stands. She is wearing a traditional Korean male
jacket, white rubber Korean gardening clogs, and a tra-
ditional Korean groom's hat with flaps on the sides that
look like Mickey Mouse ears.)

The monster towels himself off and reveals himself to be
. . . Dong-Dong!

(Korean 3 screams.)

(Evilly) Ha ha ha!

(None of the Koreans know what to do.
The Koreans begin speaking English with Asian accents
and continue to do so through the rest of the play.)

KOREAN 3 *(Improvising awkwardly)*: Oh . . . Dong-Dong!
You scare me so much!
KOREAN-AMERICAN *(To Korean 3)*: I don't care! You were
raped by our teacher. Idiot!

(Korean-American slaps Korean 3 in the face, who cries
out and falls to the ground.
Koreans 1 and 2 are delighted by this.)

Shut up, idiot! Go back to Dongdanggung!
KOREAN 3 *(Standing up)*: But I from Inchon!

(Korean-American slaps Korean 3 again, who cries out
and falls to the ground.
Koreans 1 and 2 get even more excited.)

KOREAN-AMERICAN: Idiot!

49

KOREAN 2 *(Running over to Korean-American)*: Oh, Dong-Dong! I thought you never would return.

KOREAN-AMERICAN: You were wrong, my sister, for here I am. Returned.

KOREAN 1: Oh, Dong-Dong, how we have longed for you!

KOREAN-AMERICAN: Let me tell you about a certain little fishing village in Northern Dongju. In that village is a Jew with a crap stand, and on that stand are little pieces of crap that he sells for souvenirs, and I am going to take you to that crap stand and sell you there!

(The Koreans look confused.)

KOREAN 2: Oh, Dong-Dong! I missed you!

KOREAN 3 *(Getting up)*: I hate you, Dong-Dong!

KOREAN-AMERICAN: I'm sorry, So-So, it's just that my clogs got stuck and I was trying to wipe them off and accidentally kicked you in the face!

Stand back monkeys! I'll show you how it's done!

(To audience) There is a minority rage burning inside of me. And this minority rage comes from the fact that I am a minority, and because minorities are discriminated against. And minorities are discriminated against because there is a thing in the world that is bad, and that thing is racism.

And this minority rage is raging within the minorities of the world, which can include white people if they are living in a place where they are the minority.

But back to my point, which is minority rage! I hate white people, and this is why.

(The Koreans look horrified.)

I hate white people because all minorities secretly hate them.

(The Koreans frantically shake their heads in disagreement, trying to reassure the audience that they don't hate white people.
The audience laughs.
Korean-American turns around to see what's going on and the Koreans freeze.)

If you think your best friend is black, then think again, because your best black friend hates your guts!
Your face is like a white slab of white English pudding!

(Korean 1 pushes Korean-American out of the way to make the following gracious speech. Koreans 2 and 3 kneel on either side of her, gracefully miming everything she describes. The effect should be that of a Korean Airlines promotional video welcoming Westerners to Korea.
Korean-American leaves in disgust.)

KOREAN 1: I know of a gorgeous island where all anyone ever eats is dukpuki and duk—which are special rice pastries—and dumplings with hot tea. And then they dress up in dragon costumes and run around in circles!

(The Koreans form a dragon, with Korean 2 as the head. They run around in a circle.)

KOREAN 3: I'm going to climb up the mountain to look for the silkworm!
KOREAN 1: I'm going to climb with my grandmother on my back up the mountain of Cho-Fu-San!
KOREAN 2: I have a small red bird at home that twitters!
    It goes like this:

    In the morning, I arise and look to the east
    But my eyes are filled with longing, for my lover is
        not there

Every morning I take my ivory comb and part my
    ebony hair
But my eyes are filled with longing, for my lover is
    in Dongjuksan.

*(The Koreans exit as White Person 1 storms angrily
onstage toward downstage right, with White Person 2 following her. White Person 2 tries to catch White Person 1's
arm, but she yanks it away. A row of fluorescent tubes turns
on above them.)*

WHITE PERSON 1: We have to break up.

WHITE PERSON 2: Why?

WHITE PERSON 1: First of all, you're subpar. You're of subpar intelligence.

WHITE PERSON 2: What?

WHITE PERSON 1: The world is arranged in a hierarchy with
people going from the top to the bottom, and you are pretty
high up there and so am I, but you are just a little lower
than me so that is not going to work out.

WHITE PERSON 2: What do you mean I'm of subpar
intelligence?

WHITE PERSON 1: It's just . . . I'm always watching you,
watching you like a hawk. Everyone is always watching
everyone like a fucking hawk. And I'm watching to see
what you'll do, whether you'll do something horrible and
idiotic that will make me cringe to be associated with
you. And you're always right there on the borderline of
smartness. When I say that you have subpar intelligence
I don't mean that you're stupid. I don't mean that at all.
What I mean is that you are just right on the borderline
of being smart enough for me.

WHITE PERSON 2: Like how?

WHITE PERSON 1: I don't know. Like you can follow everything I'm saying and sort of "get" everything in a way that
most people wouldn't. But what I mean is something dif-

ferent. Something much more difficult to articulate. I think your nose is too big.

WHITE PERSON 2: What?!

WHITE PERSON 1: Your nose is just way too big. I don't know, there's just something the matter with your face. When I first met you I thought you were sort of cute, because you were unknown to me and you were of the right gender and I didn't know anything about you other than that you were some guy at a party who displayed no concrete evidence of being in love with me. And that was enough for me not to scrutinize your face too closely. Also I was drunk. But then as I got to know you, I realized that your face was irreversibly inadequate. There's just something wrong with your face, I don't know how to explain it.

WHITE PERSON 2: There's something wrong with my *face*?

WHITE PERSON 1: It's the kind of face where I could possibly get used to it if I was around it all the time and it was doing things like driving me in its car and running errands for me and fetching things, but if I were to go away on a trip for a few weeks and come back to that face and see it, then I would be repulsed. I would be like, "What is wrong with his face? His nose is too big," and I would wonder how I ever let that face anywhere near me. And I wouldn't be able to look at you or even speak to you when I got home because it would be like I was sitting across from this monster, this repulsive monster that might want to touch me at some point and then I would have to push it away.

(White Person 2 walks away from White Person 1 and exits. White Person 1 follows him.

As this happens, Korean 2 enters carrying a chair and dragging a reluctant Korean-American. She sets down the chair and pushes Korean-American down on it roughly. She changes her mind, shoves Korean-American to the floor, sits in the chair herself, grabs Korean-American's hand, and leans back in the chair like an old lady, making a dying noise.

Korean-American doesn't get it, so Korean 2 coughs loudly in her face and leans back again. When Korean-American again fails to respond, Korean 2 whacks her in the head.)

KOREAN-AMERICAN *(Finally getting it)*: Grandma, you're dying!

KOREAN 2 *(Tenderly)*: Oh, Myung Bean.

KOREAN-AMERICAN: I don't want you to die, Grandma!

KOREAN 2: I know.

KOREAN-AMERICAN: I just, I can't stand the idea of you not existing in the world. It makes me think of all the ways that I was a bad granddaughter to you.

KOREAN 2: Don't worry, Myung Bean. I'm so excited I going to Jeejus house.
    Myung Bean.

KOREAN-AMERICAN: Yes, Grandma?

KOREAN 2: There is something I have say to you before I die.

KOREAN-AMERICAN: Grandma, don't . . .

KOREAN 2: No, Myung Bean, this very important. Too important for me not to say.

KOREAN-AMERICAN: Okay, Grandma, I'm listening.

KOREAN 2: Myung Bean, I see a big pain inside you.

KOREAN-AMERICAN: It's not . . . Grandma, don't worry. That's just my act I put on so that people will think I'm interesting. In reality I'm really happy. I get to do whatever I want and be totally irresponsible and selfish all the time. I love it.

KOREAN 2: Myung Bean, you can't fool Grandma.

KOREAN-AMERICAN: I'm not trying to fool you, I swear. I'm really happy.

KOREAN 2: Then why do you make such a video?

KOREAN-AMERICAN: What video?

KOREAN 2 *(Gesturing toward the back wall of the set)*: Bad video for your new play.

KOREAN-AMERICAN: How do you even know about that?

KOREAN 2: Why you ask your friend hit you in face? And then make video?

KOREAN-AMERICAN: I don't know.

(Korean 2 makes Korean hissing sound of disapproval.)

I was trying to be political.

KOREAN 2: Myung Bean, this is not a true things you are saying. You don't caring about political something. You don't even read newspaper.

KOREAN-AMERICAN: I do care!

KOREAN 2: Myung Bean, you know Grandma love you?

KOREAN-AMERICAN: Of course!

KOREAN 2: I needing talk to you about serious matter.

KOREAN-AMERICAN: Okay, Grandma.

KOREAN 2: I needing talk about Jeejus.

KOREAN-AMERICAN: Grandma, please . . .

KOREAN 2: Myung Bean, try to thinking this way. Living in world is very difficult, so people working out system of happiness for thousand and thousand of years. Young people trying live whatever they like, figuring out their own way. But look what happen! No money, stress-out, health problem, disaster! Who are you think you are to figuring out by yourself like super-genius? You are not! And being Christian has all solution handing down from generation to generation. Young people think you can drink wine, beer with your friend and it is casual, just normal thing, everybody living that way. But beer has chemical, a bad chemical that going in your brain and make it sick. When you go to hell, your arm and leg twisted with fire that is burning, and you scream but nobody hears.

(Pause.)

Myung Bean, are you happy?

KOREAN-AMERICAN: No.

KOREAN 2: Do you want to be good artist?

KOREAN-AMERICAN: Yes.

KOREAN 2: Then give up your pride, be humble. Jeejus will
help you. This is my dying wish.

Okay, Myung Bean?

(Pause.)

KOREAN-AMERICAN: Okay, Grandma. I love you.

KOREAN 2: I love you, too.

Dear Jeejus, Here is my granddaughter who I drove to
fifteen stores to look for Cabbage Patch Kid because she
wanted so badly. And here is what she say to you today.

KOREAN-AMERICAN: Dear Lord, For some reason I've always
really disliked the idea of Jesus.

(Korean 2 gives her a sharp look.)

But I'm completely miserable.

(Korean 2 smiles approvingly.)

I walk around all day feeling like I have no idea what I'm
doing and am messing everything up, and I'm constantly
tortured by the thought that other people can see what an
idiot I am and hate me for it.

KOREAN 2: Amen.

(Korean-American gives Korean 2 a look, then continues.)

KOREAN-AMERICAN: I always thought I could somehow fix
things by figuring out an intellectual system for how to
live with the maximum possible benefit to myself. But
I give up. I give up.

Dear Lord, I give my heart unto you.

KOREAN 2: Good girl. You are a good girl, Myung Bean. I love you.

(Korean 2 slumps down, dead. Koreans 1 and 3 enter singing a Korean funeral dirge, with Korean 1 miming ringing a funeral bell. Crying, Korean-American tenderly covers Korean 2's head with Korean 2's outer skirt. Korean 3 hoists Korean 2 onto her back and carries her offstage, followed by Korean 1 and Korean-American, who carries the chair offstage.

As this happens, White Person 2 walks slowly and unhappily across the stage along the back wall, while White Person 1 follows him miserably, looking contrite. They stand slightly further upstage than in their last scene. White Person 1 tries to touch White Person 2 but he jerks away. A row of fluorescent tubes turns on above them.)

WHITE PERSON 2: I was driving over a mountain range in the middle of a golf course, and what I saw was the hole. There was a hole, and it was winking at me down there in the grass and saying, "Come here, you little piece of shit. Come out here and take a crack at me."

(He looks at White Person 1 expectantly.)

WHITE PERSON 1: I want to go to Africa.

WHITE PERSON 2: I wake up in the morning with a horrible feeling, a horrible dread pushing down on me, and it's your responsibility to make me feel better about that.

(Pause.)

This is what I want from you. I want you to . . . I don't want you to have any life outside of me. I don't want you to ever go away and do something separate. I want you to be with me all the time, and for our work and pleasure to get so bound up in each other that we are never apart, having nothing uncommon and being like one person. I want to be you. I will never be happy until I literally become you, until I am negated, blanked-out, because everything that was once my individuality has become subsumed under yours, happily, forever. There are so many things I need to do. So many things. And I am terrified of them all, of each and every single one of them, and I feel weak, I feel unequipped to handle any of these things, so I want to run away. I want to do something that will make me disappear, that will make me feel and think nothing other than whatever it is that is making me disappear, which is you. And that is why I love you so much. Because if I just cling to you hard enough in my mind, I can make myself disappear and become you.

(He hugs her.

The Koreans and Korean-American enter singing a Christian song in Korean. The lyrics, "Believe in Jesus," are repeated over and over again. The White People start to exit, but the Koreans and Korean-American run over and usher them downstage center, insisting that they sit. The White People sit awkwardly on their knees next to each other, facing the audience. The Koreans sit in a semi-circle around them. Korean-American sits to the right of everyone, miming playing an acoustic guitar.

The Koreans teach the White People how to sing the song, insisting that they join in. The Koreans bust out all kinds of harmonies. The White People join in awkwardly. White Person 2 starts getting really into it and White Person 1 gives him a look.

The Koreans stop singing and abruptly but politely motion the White People offstage by waving good-bye and bowing. The White People exit, waving and bowing back, but linger at the stage left entrance to watch the scene.)

KOREAN-AMERICAN: Hey guys! I mean . . . *girls.*

(She cracks up. The Koreans laugh politely.)

I'm glad you could all make it out today.

Before we start, I want to ask you a question. Has anyone here ever experienced stress?

(The Koreans raise their hands.
White Person 1 raises her hand and White Person 2 makes her put it down.
Long, awkward pause.
Korean-American slumps over.)

KOREAN 2: What's wrong?
KOREAN-AMERICAN: I give up.
KOREAN 3: What do you give up?
KOREAN-AMERICAN: I give up on being a Christian. Also on being Korean.

(Pause. The Koreans are confused.
Korean-American springs back up, beaming.)

I'm just kidding! I wanted to loosen you guys up a little.

(She cracks up. The Koreans try to laugh but are weirded-out.)

Okay, so the thing I want to talk about today is stress. Everyone feels it, everyone knows it.

In Ecclesiastes chapter 1, the Bible says:

Vanity of vanities, saith the Preacher, vanity of vanities, all is vanity.
What profit hath a man of all his labor which he taketh under the sun?
The thing that hath been, it is that which shall be; and that which is done is that which shall be done: and there is no new thing under the sun.

59

Is there any thing whereof it may be said, See, this is new? It hath been already of old time, which was before us.

I have seen all the works that are done under the sun; and, behold, all is vanity and vexation of spirit.

And I gave my heart to know wisdom, and to know madness and folly: I perceived that this also is vexation of spirit.

For in much wisdom is much grief: and he that increaseth knowledge increaseth sorrow.

Now, this is pretty good stuff. You are schoolgirls, right? And in school you must learn all kinds of things. What kinds of things do you learn in school?

KOREAN 1: I want to be an artist!

KOREAN-AMERICAN: Okay, perfect example. What does Qoheleth mean when he says, "Vanity of vanities, all is vanity"?

KOREAN 2: He means that nothing is good and there is no hope in anything.

KOREAN-AMERICAN: That's exactly right. You think that you can work hard and be an artist and that you can create something good and new, but in reality, all is vanity because everything we try has already been done ages ago and was worthless to begin with. Don't you see? Everything is fucked-up. And it doesn't even do any good to know any of this because, as Qoheleth says, "He that increaseth knowledge increaseth sorrow."

(The Koreans are freaked-out because she said "fuck.")

KOREAN 2: Why do you swear?

KOREAN-AMERICAN: Because I forgot to tell you something. This is reverse Bible study! We are studying the Bible, but what it leads us to is my own personal teachings. I have formed a new theory.

The first step of my theory is that I don't know what I'm doing. The next step is that I'm scared. The third step is not believing in Jesus. The fourth step is . . . I don't know what the fourth step is. The fourth step is giving up. Because "vanity vanity, all is vanity."

(Korean-American breaks down crying.)

KOREAN 3: Is Jesus bad?

KOREAN 2: He's not. Jesus is good because he gives you something to live for once you realize that every other road you try is going to lead to disappointment. The reason why there are so many Christians is that believing in Jesus works.

KOREAN-AMERICAN: But Christians are evil. They're homophobic and anti-sex and racist and misogynistic and pro-life Republicans who have all the power in America and *(insert something bad the Republicans have done recently)*.

KOREAN 1: Those are white Christians, Dong-Dong. White Christians. Korean Christians are different. We are even more evil, because we add on top of the evilness of Christians the evilness of being Korean, and Koreans are the most evil nation in the world. Koreans are conservative and apolitical (except for not wanting to pay taxes) and they are greedy and anti-sex and anti-gay and racist and smell bad and talk funny and our streets smells like kimchi!

KOREAN-AMERICAN AND THE KOREANS *(Evilly)*: Ha ha ha ha ha!

KOREAN 2 *(Standing and shouting)*: Koreans, unite!

KOREAN 1 *(Making a cross with her forearms; shouting)*: Go, Christians!

KOREAN 3 *(Looking diabolically at the White People)*: They have no idea what the fuck we're doing.

(The Koreans turn their heads to look diabolically at the White People, then turn back to face the audience, drop to the floor, and roll sideways to the right until they hit the stage right wall, where they remain rolled up in little balls.

The White People look at Korean-American, who is still standing awkwardly onstage. None of them has any idea what just happened. White Person 2 begins walking toward Korean-American, who does a clumsy somersault as she exits stage right. The White People stand slightly further upstage than in their last scene. A row of fluorescent tubes turns on above them.)

WHITE PERSON 2: This is the thing about climate control. Climate control is very important.
WHITE PERSON 1: Why won't you have sex with me?

(Painful pause.)

WHITE PERSON 2: What do you mean?
WHITE PERSON 1: You never want to have sex with me anymore. It makes me hate you.
WHITE PERSON 2 *(Panicking)*: It makes me hate you, too.
WHITE PERSON 1: What's your problem? Why don't you want to have sex?

(Longer, even more painful pause.)

WHITE PERSON 2: The reason is . . . because . . . you gross me out, and I don't know why. It's just, you gross me out. You have all of these things going for you, you really do. Things that I would like to have myself. But, you're just, I don't want to fuck you.

(White Person 1 freaks out in a scary way.)

WHITE PERSON 1: I want to have a discussion with you.

WHITE PERSON 2: About what.

WHITE PERSON 1: My pens. You have to stop stealing my
pens. I like to use these very expensive roller-ball pens
and you're always stealing them and shoving them in your
pockets without the caps, and I am very disappointed in
this, it drives me crazy. It makes me want to take those
pens and jam them into the end of your penis.

(She makes a jabbing motion toward his penis.)

WHITE PERSON 2 *(Flinching backward)*: I'll try to stop doing
that, I promise.

*("All I Want for Christmas Is You," performed by Mariah
Carey from the album* Merry Christmas, *begins.*

*Korean 2 unfurls from her little ball, shaking her legs
in the air like an overturned insect. She lands in a squat
on the ground. She makes a scary monster face at the
White People and chases them offstage, scuttling like a
crab and shaking her skirts. She scuttles in place stage
left.*

*Korean 1 unfurls and scuttles stage left. Korean 3
unfurls and scuttles stage left. Korean-American scuttles
onstage wearing a traditional Korean dress over her jeans
and T-shirt and scuttles stage left.*

*The Koreans and Korean-American begin scuttling all
around the stage, making monster faces and shaking their
skirts. Korean-American, Korean 1 and Korean 3 scuttle
into the upstage right corner and scuttle with their backs
to the audience, looking like they're feeding on something.
Korean 2 head-butts them from behind, trying to get in,
but they keep her out. When the bouncy part of the song
kicks in, the Koreans and Korean-American take turns
walking downstage center to mime a gruesome suicide in
a confident manner.*

Korean 2 commits hara-kiri.

Korean 1 douses herself with kerosene and lights herself on fire.

Korean 3 stabs herself in the vagina with a knife.

Korean-American does way too much cocaine.

Korean 2 sticks a chopstick in her eye and pulls out her eyeball.

Korean 1 cuts off two of her fingers with a pair of scissors, then cuts off her tongue and stabs herself in the eyes.

Korean 3 drinks a bottle of beer, smashes the bottle over her knee, and uses the broken bottle to cut her wrists.

Korean-American puts her head in an oven and resumes scuttling.

Korean 2 cuts around her jawline, peels off her face, rolls it up, smokes it like a cigarette and resumes scuttling.

Korean 1 cradles her imaginary baby, then shoots her baby in the head and then herself and resumes scuttling.

Korean 3 cuts off her breast, bites a chunk out of it, throws her breast into the audience, spits the chunk at the audience, and resumes scuttling.

They all scuttle together.

The White People enter with chairs and shoo the Koreans offstage, shaking their chairs at the Koreans like lion tamers. The White People sit center stage. A row of fluorescent tubes turns on above them. They sit for a long time, looking miserable.)

Why is this happening to us?

WHITE PERSON 1: I want to talk about something besides our relationship.

WHITE PERSON 2: Okay, what do you want to talk about?

WHITE PERSON 1: I want to talk about politics.

WHITE PERSON 2: Okay.

WHITE PERSON 1: I want there to be some kind of political situation between us. I want us to be some kind of political rivals or something.

WHITE PERSON 2: Okay.

(Pause.)

I'm the Vice President of the United States . . . and you are some guy who I want to hire for the government. Some white guy.

WHITE PERSON 1: Okay, let's start.

WHITE PERSON 2: I want you to be my Communications Director of the United States of America. I am your handler and I have been designated your handler to close the deal of you becoming Communications Director. Do you accept my offer?

WHITE PERSON 1: I do not wish to be your Communications Director.

WHITE PERSON 2: Why not.

WHITE PERSON 1: I've done that before.

WHITE PERSON 2: Come on, I want you to be Communications Director. Also, you'll be important. And also I just want you to because I've been designated as your handler to get you to be Communications Director.

WHITE PERSON 1: I do not wish to be your Communications Director. I want some other job in the U.S. Government.

(The Koreans and Korean-American enter and stand in a row in front of the White People, blocking them from the audience's view. The Koreans and Korean-American look at the audience in silence.)

KOREAN-AMERICAN AND THE KOREANS *(In unison)*: Hello. Thank you all for coming here today. Your eyes are not worthy of . . . I mean, my face is not worthy of the strain on your eyes to look at it. My ears are not worth the effort of . . . um. My voice is not worthy of the effort of your ears to listen to it. It breaks my heart that it's hard for me to say I'm sorry.

I don't know what the white people are doing in this show. I don't even know what the Asian people are doing. All I know is that I come up with all this racist shit, and when minorities get mad I'm like, "Go to hell, you unfashionably angry minorities, this is my sophisticated critique of racism that you are too stupid to understand." But the truth is, if you're a minority and you do super-racist stuff against yourself, then the white people are like, "Oh, you're a 'cool' minority," and they treat you like one of them.

I want to be white. I want to get really annoyed whenever anyone brings up race. I want to say things like, "I don't think of people in terms of race. I find it more interesting to focus on our shared human experience." I want to deny that anything is racist short of slavery and genocide.

When minorities attack, white women are always like, "What about the fact that I'm a woman?" but nobody really gives a shit about that. You spend all this time obsessing over your looks and being jealous of other women, and then you bust out your self-righteous feminism like it's some cherry for the top of your cream puff.

I love the white patriarchy with all my heart because I'm ambitious and want power. My whole mentality is identical in structure to that of a sexist, racist, homosexual white male. People think of me as this empowered Asian female, but really, I'm just a fucking white guy.

And some of you may be thinking, "Oh man, this is a speech about how white people suck. This is so much less complicated and interesting than all the other parts of the show that weren't just about race." But don't worry. If enough white people hate it, I'll cut it.

I apologize for bringing shame upon my country.

(They bow and shuffle backward offstage, parting like a curtain, with two exiting stage right and two exiting stage left, revealing the White People.

*All of the rows of fluorescent tubes turn on at once.
Someone turns off the air conditioner, which has been
whirring noisily throughout the show.)*

WHITE PERSON 1: I want to go to Africa.

WHITE PERSON 2: There is a drama between you and I.

WHITE PERSON 1: I'm going to make some toast.

WHITE PERSON 2: Why?

WHITE PERSON 1: Because I have to eat breakfast.

WHITE PERSON 2: Why?

WHITE PERSON 1: Because it's healthy to eat a good breakfast, and I'm trying to be healthy.

WHITE PERSON 2: Why are you trying to be healthy? Why
don't you just be an alcoholic like me?

WHITE PERSON 1: Are you an alcoholic?

WHITE PERSON 2: Yes.

WHITE PERSON 1: That's bad!

WHITE PERSON 2: No. I'm not an alcoholic.

WHITE PERSON 1: You're an alcoholic! That's bad!

WHITE PERSON 2: I'm not an alcoholic! I just like to party!

WHITE PERSON 1: Stop being an alcoholic, boyfriend!

WHITE PERSON 2: No! I'm not an alcoholic!

WHITE PERSON 1: Listen, you! You have to stop being an
alcoholic, because that is not good for our relationship!

WHITE PERSON 2 *(Screaming)*: I'm not an alcoholic!
(Normal voice) This is very exciting, all of this talk
about alcoholism.

WHITE PERSON 1 *(Screaming really loudly)*: GO OUT OF
THIS ROOM!

(White Person 2 exits.)

Now come back in!

(White Person 2 reenters.)

WHITE PERSON 2: Hi.
WHITE PERSON 1: Hi.
WHITE PERSON 2: What are you doing?
WHITE PERSON 1: Thinking.
WHITE PERSON 2: It's almost three in the morning.
WHITE PERSON 1: It is?
WHITE PERSON 2: I woke up and you weren't there.
What are you thinking about?
WHITE PERSON 1: About you being an alcoholic.
Ugh. No.
Go out and then come back in.
WHITE PERSON 2: Okay.

(White Person 2 exits again and reenters.)

Hey.
WHITE PERSON 1: Hey.
WHITE PERSON 2: What are you doing?
WHITE PERSON 1: Nothing. Thinking.
WHITE PERSON 2: It's almost three in the morning.
WHITE PERSON 1: It is?
WHITE PERSON 2: I want to switch.
WHITE PERSON 1: Okay.

(White Person 1 exits.
White Person 2 is excited. He sits in White Person 1's
chair and waits eagerly.
White Person 1 enters.)

Hey.
WHITE PERSON 2: Hey!
WHITE PERSON 1: No, this doesn't work.
WHITE PERSON 2: Why do I always have to be the pathetic one?!
WHITE PERSON 1: Just go!

(White Person 2 exits sullenly.

White Person 2 reenters and leans in an unnatural-looking pose against the back wall.)

WHITE PERSON 2: Hey.
WHITE PERSON 1: Hey.
WHITE PERSON 2: What are you doing?
WHITE PERSON 1: Nothing.
WHITE PERSON 2: It's three in the morning.
WHITE PERSON 1: Really?
WHITE PERSON 2: I woke up in our bed and rolled over to see you and you weren't there in our bed that we share together.

(Pause.)

Are you okay?

(White Person 2 gets suspicious. He looks around. He "sees" her coffee cup, mimes bringing it to his nose, smelling it.)

Hey!

Hey, there's alcohol in here! You stupid alcoholic!
WHITE PERSON 1: No, stop it.
WHITE PERSON 2: Alcoholic!
WHITE PERSON 1: I don't really give a fuck about that. Let's talk about my inside, my inner private life. When I'm sitting in the room with you, sitting right in front of you, you can see what I'm doing. But the thing is, you don't know what I'm really doing because the second I walk out of this room, you don't have any idea what the fuck I'm doing. I say I'm going to the bathroom, and you can imagine what I would be doing, but what if that's not what I'm doing at all? What if I'm not fucking going to the fucking bathroom? What then?

WHITE PERSON 2: What are you doing?

WHITE PERSON 1: What if I—what if you think that I'm sitting across from you, listening to you, but instead I'm not listening at all and instead I'm thinking about all the nasty sexual things I'm going to do to your stuffed turtle. And I had cut a hole into the belly of your turtle and then when I said I was going to the bathroom, I went into our bedroom and strapped on a dildo and fucked this hole in the turtle's stomach until I came, and then went back down to where you were and sat down and put my napkin on my lap and was like, "Okay, I'm back."

WHITE PERSON 2: You have to stop drinking!

WHITE PERSON 1: Why.

WHITE PERSON 2: Because I can't be your boyfriend anymore if you keep drinking! You have to stop drinking completely!

WHITE PERSON 1: Why.

WHITE PERSON 2: Because, do you know that the world and people are not what they are, in many parts of the country? They are something completely other than what they are. Especially in America, but we see it all over the world. We see it in the movies and things, people acting all crazy and being all depressed and weird, and it's like, "Ooh, what a depressing world and culture we live in. What an existential state!" But really none of that even really exists inside of us. None of us is really romantic and crazy and exciting. It's just that the chemicals in alcohol does something to the chemicals in our brains and bodies and makes things go haywire, so that even if we're not drinking much, even if we have just one wine or beer, then our chemistry is all haywire and we are no longer who we are. Do you understand that?

WHITE PERSON 1: I want to go to Africa.

WHITE PERSON 2: Why do you keep saying that?

WHITE PERSON 1: Because I want to go in the banana tree. There is monkeys in the banana trees and they are—it is a big green banana tree with many yellow bananas on it, and the monkeys are sitting in the tree eating the bananas, and they are smiling. They are very happy to be in a banana tree. And that is what I want to do is go to Africa and climb up into the banana tree and eat bananas with those monkeys and be happy. I don't want to talk about any of this stuff!

WHITE PERSON 2: Well, I want to go to . . . Strawberry Patch Grove.

WHITE PERSON 1: There is no such place.

WHITE PERSON 2: Yes there is. There's a Strawberry Patch Grove where everyone wears hats that look like muffins and they carry around baskets filled with muffins and strawberries. And everyone wears aprons, even the men, and they have these little rubber clogs that they wear. And they sit in their . . . each of them has a little strawberry patch in their backyard with a table and an umbrella shaped like a teacup, and they sit at those tables and eat ice cream in the sunshine. And that's where I'm going to go. I'm going to leave you here alone in this apartment and go to Strawberry Patch Grove.

Are you happy that you're white?

WHITE PERSON 1: I don't think about it that much.

(Pause.)

WHITE PERSON 2: You know what's awesome?

WHITE PERSON 1: What.

WHITE PERSON 2: Being white.

WHITE PERSON 1: Being white?

WHITE PERSON 2: Yes, it's awesome. Isn't it?

WHITE PERSON 1: I guess I never thought of it. And when I do think of it I feel like an asshole.

WHITE PERSON 2: You shouldn't feel like an asshole. Being white is great.

WHITE PERSON 1: I guess so.

71

WHITE PERSON 2: What are all the white things that are great? Snow. Marshmallows. Cream sauce. Paper.

WHITE PERSON 1: We're not really white like that, though.

I think I lost ten dollars.

WHITE PERSON 2: Oh shit, that sucks.

Did you enter it into Quicken?

WHITE PERSON 1: Yes, but obviously there's no receipt.

WHITE PERSON 2: Do you know that you're the most beautiful person I've ever known in my life? There is so much beauty in you, I can't stand it. You are a wonder. And I can't remember, I can't remember what it was to love you.

WHITE PERSON 1 *(Crying)*: You're not . . . that's not true. That's not true what you're saying about there being so much beauty inside me. Look into my eyes and try to see even though I know you can't. I am a monster. I am a fucking monster. There is *nothing there.*

WHITE PERSON 2: This is why I love you. I know what you're like on the outside—the part that everyone else sees and runs away from—but I don't care about any of that. I can only see the things that are the most beautiful about you. For me, you radiate a kind of halo of hope, a hope that the world might be worth living in if it was capable of creating someone as beautiful and worth loving as you. And I know that you hate it, that you hate being loved this much and would do anything to escape it, and I think you should if you want to, but the fact of my love will always exist and I'm happy about it. I will always miss you. I will always see things in the world that I love and want to show them to you. I will always want everything good for you. And it's such a relief, it's such a fucking relief to know that I can feel that for another human being—that my capacity to feel love is vast enough that I can look through all of the earthly claptrap around your soul and see things that even you have no idea are there.

(White Person 1 turns her back on him.)

I am so much smarter than you will ever know. You have no idea what I'm up to, because what I'm showing you never reflects what is actually happening in my mind. I never loved you or anyone else. The reason why I act pathetic, why I let you treat me like shit is because I don't care. It's like my relationship to alcohol. I don't spend a lot of time strategizing about how to make alcohol *like* me, I just want to get it. Oh I see you with perfect clarity, and I promise that the contempt you feel for me is a dwarfed, microscopic fraction of the contempt I feel for you.

(White Person 1 looks at him.)

And I'm saying all of this to save myself from the utter terror of the idea of living in the world without you, the utter terror of the idea that I felt love, that it was real, and that it's something I will never feel again.

(White Person 2 breaks down crying.)

WHITE PERSON 1 *(Crying)*: Last night, I had a dream. I had a dream that I went out into the hall at three in the morning and you were there, floating on a white cloud. And I stepped onto the white cloud and we went to couples counseling. And I dreamed that we had health insurance and that the health insurance paid for it. And in my dream, we went to couples counseling once a week for a year, and our health insurance paid for all of it, and each of us also went to individual counseling once a week, which the health insurance also paid for. And I dreamed that we both stopped drinking and smoking and using drugs and caffeine and began to eat healthy and exercise and get lots of sleep, and that suddenly the world opened up before us and many of our bad feelings went away. I dreamed that we learned how to be humble and realistic, and that our newfound humility enabled us to develop our true gifts to a greater extent than we could when we were beating ourselves up to do better. I dreamed that we both stopped hating ourselves enough to value each other's love and look after it, and that we grew old together, and had grandchildren, and children, and things like that. It was the most wonderful dream I've ever had.

(Pause.)

WHITE PERSON 2: It doesn't have to just be a dream! It can be true! We can call up one of our friends and ask them for the name of a therapist.
WHITE PERSON 1: Okay.

(He holds out his phone.
They stare at the phone.
"Held," performed by Smog from the album Knock Knock, *begins.*
When the beat drops, lights out.)

END OF PLAY

Pullman, WA

For Mac Wellman

Production History

Pullman, WA was originally produced by Young Jean Lee's
Theater Company. It premiered in March 2005 at Performance Space 122 in New York. It was written and directed by
Young Jean Lee; the lighting design was by Eric Dyer. It was
co-created and performed by:

TOM	Thomas Bradshaw
PETE	Pete Simpson
TORY	Tory Vazquez

Characters

TOM
PETE
TORY

Note

"Pete," "Tory" and "Tom" were the names of the performers of *Pullman, WA* in its original production at Performance Space 122. The characters should be named after whoever is playing them.

A bare stage except for two chairs off to the side facing the audience. This is the "giving up" area, that is, the place where the characters go when they've given up. The house lights remain up throughout. There are no lighting or sound changes. Everyone wears ordinary street clothes.

In general, lines between characters are directed both to each other and the audience.

Pete enters.

PETE: I see you out there.

I see you out there and I can see that you are all different kinds of people.

You are all going through different kinds of things.

Some of you may be happy. Others of you may be in hell. I don't know. But what I do know is that I know how to live.

(Pause.)

I don't know what all different kinds of people are like.

There are too many kinds, so I don't know what each one is like.

You are sitting in your seat. You have come to the theater, and you are sitting in your seat, and you are someone.

Everything you are, sitting in that seat and being where you are, is what you are.

I wish I knew what it was like to be you.

But you are sitting out there, in your seat. And, probably, you are listening to and watching me.

What are you doing here?

I don't even know why I'm asking these things, but somehow it seems important. It seems important but maybe it's not because I'm going to tell you how to live.

I know how to live.

I don't know if you ever felt this way, but sometimes life feels confusing. For me, personally, a lot of times, life feels confusing. A lot of times in my life I have felt that I did not know what I was doing and that everything was fucked-up. That is a familiar feeling for me, so I know what that feels like.

And during those times when I felt so unhappy and confused, I would wish that someone would tell me what to do. That I could pick up a recipe book, and it would be a recipe book for life, which would tell me what I should do to live a good life and be happy.

There are books and people who claim to give you these things, but none of them work.

But now I know, I've figured out how to live, and this is not a joke.

We are in this room. We are in this room together and I am speaking to you, and I am going to tell you how to live.

I am confused now.

But now I am clear again.

I keep coming back to the main point, which is that you are sitting in your chair and I don't know who you are or what you are like. But I know how to live, so I can tell you that. And maybe you already know how to live, so this will be old news to you, but no human being is perfect so maybe it will still be useful for you.

Okay, so the first thing for you to know is that *you* are *you*. Some of you already know this. Some of you know it so well that you don't even have to think about it. You have always been you and that was that.

But for some of you, and I know how it feels because I'm like this too, the idea that you are you is more shaky.

You think that you are too unproductive or do stupid things, and this makes you not you.

Okay, I'm not being very clear. Let me try to give you a personal example. For me, I have never felt like I was me. There was always something wrong with who I was so that I was always thinking of myself as some future-existing person, someone who—like an outline of some-one—oh shit, it's hard to talk about this stuff.

Okay. There is this idea that some people have that they don't count if they are fucked-up in some way.

Like this idea of being fat. If you're fat, then you're not who you're supposed to be. You're supposed to be thin. So when you're fat, it's like you don't count, like you're not you. Does that make sense?

It is very difficult to believe . . .

(Pause.)

Do you know what other people look like to me? They look so sure of themselves, so settled in their identity. "I am this, and this is my life, and it is good." A kind of absolute certainty about themselves that enables them to be completely honest in everything they say. You know, it's a weird thing, but I always assume that the people I talk to are being one hundred percent honest with me. Even though I know that I myself am frequently dishonest, I believe that other people are honest because I feel they have nothing to lie about. But that seems kind of unlikely, huh?

Sorry I'm taking so long to get to the how to live part, but this is all part of it. This is all how it gets set up.

So anyway, when you look at other people and they seem to have such stable identities, the fact of the matter is that you have a stable identity as well.

I know you don't want it, but you have it and it's there.

There are all kinds of gifts that get doled out in this life.

I look out there at you and there's a whole range of physical graces that got bestowed upon you.

And being born with certain gifts makes life a lot easier in many ways. If you were born beautiful, and rich, and smart, and charismatic, to a loving family, then you are not going to endure the same kind of suffering as someone who was born ugly, and poor, and awkward, and stupid, to an abusive family.

And a lot of this has to do with social skills. Social skills are one of the most important things in the planet. It is possible for someone born with few gifts, but gifted with social skills, to be better off than someone who is born with many gifts but is bad at social skills.

And by social skills I don't mean the ability to talk a lot and schmooze at parties. By social skills I mean an intuitive sense of how to act around other people so that they want to keep being around you. Like if you're in a subway station and someone is sitting at one end of an empty bench, and you're the kind of person who would go sit right next to that person instead of leaving at least two or three spaces in between you, then you're pretty much fucked for life. Even homeless people know better than to do that.

But then again I don't know how much looks and things factor in.

(Pause.)

I feel like I'm not doing a good job of explaining things.

Misery is not always such a straightforward proposition of you saying, "I feel miserable." Sometimes it comes out in other weird ways, too. You know those health problems you have, those weird health problems that the doctors can't diagnose? The inexplicable skin problems, back problems, knee problems, problems with your genitals, things like that? Chances are pretty high that those are psychosomatic.

You may not know it, but some of you hate yourselves. You hate yourselves for not being the thing you're supposed to be, for not having the life you're supposed to have. And the distance between you and that thing you're supposed to be is killing you. It makes you break out in these weird health problems and it makes you do bad things that are bad to yourself.

A lot of us seem to have contempt for happiness. It's cooler to be destructive and chaotic and romantic and extreme—and that's always what I've valued my whole life and still do. I love all that stuff—the violent, the crazy, the extreme. I think it's great. But the thing is, it has a negative backfire that leaves you feeling like shit.

But let's talk about something important, which is the idea of suffering. When I think of suffering in the world, I think of the obvious things. People who are being tortured, victims of natural disasters, people living under oppressive regimes in poverty-stricken countries, kids who are being abused . . . all that stuff sucks.

But these are not things that you're dealing with. There is all kinds of self-inflicted pain that you are doing to yourself, and some of you have no idea that you are doing it.

The biggest self-torturing device I see around me are people having obsessive bad thoughts. Whenever you make a mistake or something bad happens, you start obsessing about it over and over in your mind in this private internal freak-out. But think about it this way. If you saw some parent relentlessly picking on their kid in the same way that you pick on yourself whenever everything's not perfect in your life, you would probably feel really fucking afraid for that kid.

We have this idea that we need to whip ourselves into shape, without realizing it's the whipping that's causing us to be fucked-up in the first place.

And stop thinking of all of this as being for pussies and still trying to cling to all your stubborn little notions about your current situation. If it worked for you that would be one thing, but it doesn't even work.

Now, this theory that I have . . .

Okay, I've been talking for a while, and much of it has been repetitive and a good portion probably unconvincing.

Here is one convincing thing. As an experiment, try doing the following things for one day:

1. Eating only healthy food.
2. Getting some exercise.
3. Not drinking alcohol.
4. Going to bed early.

Then wake up the next morning. You will probably feel better!

Everyone is born with *something*, and it's important to develop whatever parts of yourself you want to develop. Like if you're good at science, it's a good thing to study science more and more to the point where you're getting better at science and knowing more about it.

Wow, that's a boring example.

But you get the general idea. And it's not a moral thing. It's just that you're hurting yourself. You keep doing things that hurt yourself—things that you might not even suspect as hurting yourself. You drink too much, you have unprotected sex, you stay in bad relationships, you let yourself get overburdened with responsibilities, you don't get enough sleep, you smoke, you watch too much TV, you don't do the things you want to spend your time doing.

It doesn't matter, all this judging that goes on between people, all this intuitive sensing of weakness and criticism of it. There is no big shining ideal that matters, either. The only thing that matters is feeling good. And if it makes you feel good to help people and make a difference in the world, then you should do that. And fuck anyone who says that you're an asshole if you're not out there tending the sick and feeding the poor. That's just another unrealistic delusion of what people are supposed to be.

If you can wake up sober after a good night's sleep, it should feel good. I guess that's the meaning of life. Being able to walk down the street without physical pain and without being chased by the police. If you're being tortured, if you have squalid poverty, if you're some kid cowering in the basement as their psycho parent rampages throughout the house, it's hard to feel good. Feeling good is a luxury. Stop torturing yourself.

But now I'm being repetitive again. Let me tell you something new.

Okay, this isn't new at all. It's going to be exactly what I said before in a different format, but it's an important point to hammer in.

(He holds up his left fist.)

This is you.

(He holds up his right fist above his left fist.)

And this is the you that you're supposed to be.

And this is what you do whenever you feel like you're not meeting the expectations of your higher self.

(He slowly pounds his right fist into the palm of his left hand with an agonized expression.

Tory runs onstage and shoves Pete to the floor, smiling happily.

Pete goes to the giving up area.)

TORY *(To the audience, smiling)*: You are sitting in the middle of a giant puffball.

It's your birthday, and the sun is out. The sun is warming the outside of your puffball.

You have . . . all your friends look like mushrooms, except for the ones who look like unicorns.

There is a long drama with one of your friends. She was originally your sister, but then you were separated by wickedness and she flew away, I mean she died, she was killed, and flew away to heaven. But then years later you were reunited through a chain of unforeseen circumstances.

It was a great birthday party. We blew up the pool and put in the waterslide and had watermelon cake. It is summer.

You saw an old man in the middle of the road and invited him to the party, and it turned out he was a magician, so he did tricks. He made people's heads float on top of the pool like apples without hurting them.

And then we played all of our owl music on our owl record players and played the same song on both players so it was like double stereo.

Last summer we had some good parties. We tied all the unicorns together and had a unicorn race where nobody could win because they were all chained together, which was fine because unicorns are not a competitive animal.

Last summer there was also a troll who kept eating people, and we had to—he ate a chunk out of *your* unicorn—and he had to be killed.

We are not afraid to kill if the need arises.

The biggest thing about us is that we are strong. We are a strong people and nothing can crush us.

PETE *(From the giving up area, to the audience)*: You are a failure!

(All of the following, until Tom's entrance, is directed at the audience. Tory smiles happily throughout.)

TORY: You are in a canoe on a lake, with swans floating all around you. The swans are quacking out all kinds of songs to you. The swans spell out the words to the songs by swimming in formation with their bodies so you can remember the lyrics and sing them to yourself later on.

PETE: Everyone thinks you suck!

TORY: You are flying in a rainbow-colored balloon in the sky that is filled with jackrabbits. The jackrabbits keep jumping out of the balloon, hitting the earth, and bouncing back up to wave at you. Sometimes they bounce off the side of the balloon and fly through space until they bounce off the moon and ping-pong through the stars.

PETE: Nobody will ever truly love you and you will never truly love anyone.

TORY: You are on the inside of a stapler. The outward casing is protecting you until it is time to do your job, which is simple and straightforward.

PETE: You tell people you like their art when really you think it sucks.

TORY: You constantly talk shit about people behind their backs, even people you don't know.

PETE: You act like you're still in high school.

TORY: You are flying over a rainbow on the back of a unicorn. As you get close to the rainbow you can see that it is made of millions of smiling otters. The otters are hooting in welcome, and the hooting is filling your head and pushing out your brain until it falls out and nothing is left but their soft hooting.

PETE: You reveal deeply personal information about your friends to other people.

TORY: You want to be famous.

PETE: You accuse other people of wanting to be famous.

TORY: You are lying in your bed, surrounded by angels. The pattern from your blanket has floated up into the air and the angels are blowing it back and forth at each other above your bed. You fall asleep to the image of plaid floating in front of your eyes.

(Pete leaves the giving up area and stands next to Tory.)

PETE: You pretend to be interested in boring things in social situations.
TORY: You are constantly trying to make yourself a better person, but this never involves helping anyone else.
PETE: You're kind of unexpectedly prissy.
TORY: You have a fake laugh that you use all the time.
PETE: You are full of self-righteous political wrath but do nothing about it.
TORY: You are much more mundane than you lead others to believe.
PETE: You are obsessed with saving small sums of money.
TORY: You think your bad moods should swallow the whole world.
PETE: You're so judgmental of other people, it's kind of awful. Who the fuck cares, why can't you just leave people the fuck alone? Everyone is doing their best, they're just trying to do whatever they can to live an okay life and feel a little better about themselves every once in a while, but you're so mean about it!

(Pete returns to the giving up area.
Tory goes through the audience directing each of her following lines to a different person, still smiling.)

TORY: You have taken on way more responsibility than you can handle.
There are a million things you need to do that are not getting done.
Other people are not helping you in the ways that they should be.

Your feelings of anxiety are fucking up your focus and productivity.

You keep wasting time that you cannot afford to lose.

You are incompetent.

You have no idea what you're doing.

You've fooled other people into thinking you're an adult.

People are trusting you to do a good job.

The whole premise behind what you're doing sucks.

You've made a series of incredibly bad decisions.

Everyone is mad at you.

(To the whole audience) This is going to be a total disaster.

(Tom enters.)

TOM: I am an angel of the Lord.

I have flown vast distances over pure white fields.

I have come to bring you rest.

I will stand watch over you in the night.

I will guard your path in the daylight hours.

Have no more fear.

I will shelter and protect you.

Amen.

TORY *(Going to the giving up area)*: This is a total disaster.

TOM *(To Pete, Tory and the audience)*: Stop freaking out.

I know you feel totally scared and confused right now but it's okay, I can help you.

It's okay.

Calm down.

You are not a failure.

Calm down.

I don't want you to get so unhappy like this anymore.

There were two shepherds, and the Lord asked them to protect and watch over his lambs in the field.

The shepherds said, "Yes, Lord, I will obey," and tended the lambs with gentleness and care.

But soon the shepherds grew weary of their task and began to beat and flay the lambs with their staffs.

The Lord descended upon them and asked, "Did I not ask you to protect and watch over my lambs in the field?"

"Yes, Lord," said the shepherds.

"And did you not say to me, 'Yes, Lord, I will obey?'" asked the Lord.

"Yes, Lord," said the shepherds.

"Then why do you not obey?" asked the Lord. "Why do you beat and flay my lambs with your staffs?"

"We did not beat and flay your lambs with our staffs," lied the shepherds.

The Lord replied—

PETE (*Leaving the giving up area; to the audience*): You know what? Fuck this!

You are fucked-up! You might not know it, but you are. And you think that everything that goes wrong in your life is because other people are fucking things up, but actually it's because *you're* fucked-up!

Fuck you!

TORY (*From the giving up area, to the audience*): Go fuck yourselves!

(*All of the following, until Tom's speech, is directed at the audience.*)

PETE: You are alone!

TORY: You are completely alone!

PETE: Nobody can ever feel what you feel!

TORY (*Leaving the giving up area*): If you looked into your mind you would see mess upon mess!

PETE: There is nothing but failure!

TORY: I can't help you!

PETE: Nobody can help you! You should have been born different!

90

(Tom is horrified.)

TOM *(To the audience)*: I'm the King of All Kings.
   Bring your sufferings unto me.
   Speak unto me your troubles, child.
   (To Pete and Tory, indignantly) There's a bad thing inside you, and you don't even know it.
   There's . . .

(Tom suddenly howls in pain. Tory and Pete follow suit.
   Tory calms down. As she speaks the following lines, Pete and Tom become happy.)

TORY: It's okay. It's . . . there's a field. A green field. And on that field are unicorns, white unicorns. They are soft and gentle and they are singing through their nose a silent song, an airy whistle, and there are white clouds in the sky. This is the way the world works. Green field, white unicorns, blue sky, white clouds. You are safe. I will protect you.

TOM: I will protect you from all harm.
   No harm will come to you.
   If you deliver your heart unto me, you will be forgiven.
   (Pointing to a person in the audience) Stop crying, child. Rise and walk again.
   Rise up.
   Have no fear.

PETE: A few minutes from now, an army of soldiers will come marching over the side of that hill, and you will be saved. All you have to do is wait behind this rock. Keep very still. Put your head down, like this.

(He hides his head with his arms.
   Tory hides her head with her arms.)

I can still see you! Hold very still. Don't look up. Don't look up at that—

TOM: Have no fear. *I* know you feel alone. *I* know you feel that you are surrounded by traitors.

PETE: Whatever you did, however bad it was, it's okay. It's okay. *I* forgive you.

TOM: *I* want to help you. *I'm* going to help you.

PETE *(To Tom)*: Maybe they don't need help.

TORY *(To the audience)*: You are a loser. You're a loser because you were born that way. You will never be anything other than what you are. This is the way the world works. I am helping you by telling the truth. You are a loser and you will lose.

PETE *(To Tory)*: Ow.

(Pause.)

Ow!

TORY: Shut up.

PETE *(To Tom)*: Help!

TOM *(To the audience)*: I will never leave you alone.

(To Pete and Tory) You guys are assholes.

TORY: I don't care.

PETE *(To the audience)*: What if everything started spinning until it became a little round owl face on a record player? Would that make you feel better?

Imagine it. A little round owl face on a record player that goes around and around without stopping, forever.

TORY *(To the audience)*: If you drive out far enough into the fog, eventually you'll go flying off into another world. You have no idea what that place is like.

TOM: I want to say something.

(Pause.)

(To Pete and Tory, angrily) You are sitting in the middle of a lake, and the lake is on fire! The trees around the lake are on fire, and you are on fire!

(To the audience) And everything spins out the wrong way and then goes back in. It swirls and swirls, spinning in an endless sea of light, and then the bull comes over the horizon with its little horns and saves everybody, because that is the nature of the animal. That is the nature of the animal within.

Let me tell you about my childhood.

When I was a kid, I wasn't allowed to go trick-or-treating.

When I became a young man, I wanted my penis to turn into a turtle, but it never did.

I think you need my help.

I will save you.

It's okay.

It's okay I will save you.

There's a place in the woods, and we can go there.

PETE *(Dreamily)*: There's a fog at the end of the road.

TOM *(To Pete, angrily)*: You don't know what that place is like! You have a bad thing inside you, and you don't even know it!

(To the audience) Come unto me.

I am you are the meek and the lamb.

Everything will be okay.

Everything will be okay. I know things.

I know . . . things.

I don't know shit.

PETE *(To the audience, businesslike)*: We'll do it in steps.

TOM *(Falling apart)*: I don't know. I don't know shit.

TORY *(To the audience, businesslike)*: This is how to live.

(Pause. Tom silently freaks out.)

PETE: Be good.
TORY: Be good.
PETE: Do things.
TORY: Do things.
PETE: Don't do bad things.

TORY: Don't do bad things.

TOM: OW! OW! OW!

> I fucked up!
> *I* fucked up!
> *(To Pete)* Sorry.
> *(To Tory)* Sorry.

(Tom goes to the giving up area.)

PETE: Eat healthy.

TORY: Eat healthy and exercise.

PETE: Don't smoke.

TORY: Don't drink.

PETE: Get lots of sleep.

TORY: What else.

PETE: Don't use drugs.

TORY: What else.

PETE: Don't do it because of morality. Do it because it's selfish for you. Do it because it brings lots of good rewards to you personally.

TORY: Okay what else.

PETE: I don't know.

TORY: Do what makes you feel good.

PETE: Don't hurt anyone.

TORY: Hurting people is an egotistical high.

PETE: Which has a negative backfire on *you.*

TOM *(Leaving the giving up area)*: All right. All right.

> There was a pack of wolves with two female wolves in it. One was powerful and the other had no power. One day, the weak female gave birth to a bunch of baby wolves, and for the first time in her life she knew what it felt like to be happy. That night, the powerful female went into the mother wolf's den, dragged out her pups one by one right in front of her, and killed them.

(Pause. Nobody likes his story. He tries again.)

You were sitting in a white field, and everything was white. The sky was white. There was nothing but emptiness and white and quiet.

PETE *(Happily)*: And unicorns.

TOM *(To Pete, angrily)*: There were no unicorns there!

(Pete makes an irritated gesture.)

PETE: The unicorns are flying over the rainbow!

TOM *(To Pete)*: I must confess.

You are a bad person.

(Pete gets mad.)

TORY *(Interrupting them, preventing a fight)*: You are in a spaceship made of donkey balls. You are flying around and around the Earth. The stewardesses are serving you cocktails that are red and green and blue and purple, and you are looking out your window.

TOM *(Pitifully)*: I don't see it.

I think I'm dying.

I'm dying.

My liver. My penis.

TORY *(To the audience)*: I can see you out there. I can see you sitting out there with your little pinched lips and your prissy face, sitting there all high and mighty with your little squeezed-up, pinched-up prissy disapproving face going, "I don't like this." Well, the reason why you're sitting up there all unhappy with your little, pinched, disapproving lips is not because what *we're* doing sucks, but because *you're* lacking. You're lacking in something. We all know people like this, who have some part of their brain that's gone dead, who can't understand anything and want to be left alone in their little bubble of vacuity to carry on their stupid life without ever having to think about anything, ever. You're a judgmental, negative priss

who accuses other people of being judgmental and negative. Why don't you go home, you fucking hypocrite.

PETE: I am on an underwater planet in the belly of a whale,
which is populated by fish. The fish go to school, where
they learn about fishing. There is a glass tank in the belly
of the whale, and every time the whale eats a fish the
carcass comes drifting down into the tank for anatomy
class.

TOM: You are on a field in a forest.

TORY: You are on a field in a forest and you are singing, you
are riding a horse.

TOM *(To the audience, kindly)*: Just . . . go ahead and be
pathetic. It's okay. It's not pathetic.

TORY *(To the audience, very mean)*: You should have been
born different.

TOM: It's not pathetic.

TORY: It's completely pathetic.

PETE: Shut up!

TORY: What's wrong?

PETE: I didn't get to say any of the things I wanted to say!

TOM: Don't say them.

TORY: Shut up! Everyone shut up!

PETE: You shut up! I didn't get to say anything!

TOM: You can say anything you want.

TORY: Say it now.

TOM: Say it!

PETE: I want to say . . .

TORY: What? Say it!

TOM: Say something!

PETE: I . . . know something.

TOM: What?

PETE: I know . . . how to live.

TORY: How do you do it?

PETE: Somebody else say it.

TOM: This is how to live.

TORY: Be born different.

TOM: Somebody else say it.
PETE: I'll say it.
TOM: Say it!

(Pause.)

TORY *(Going to the giving up area)*: I think you just have to be born different.

(Pete and Tom look at each other and awkwardly get into "Jesus/God" positions, standing next to each other facing the audience. Pete is Jesus and Tom is God.
    All of the following lines are directed to the audience until Tom's first sudden howl of pain.)

PETE: Fear not, for I will walk upon the land.
TOM: I will walk upon the land, in the hills and the valley below.
PETE: I will walk upon the land and shout my name.
TOM: I will shout my name in the desert.
PETE: Over the plains and in the valley, you will hear my name echoing.
TOM: You will hear my name echoing into the hills.
PETE: You will hear my name echoing and fall down.
TOM: You will fall down groveling upon the earth.
PETE: You will weep and curse my name.
TOM: You will curse my name and I will smite you down.
PETE: I will swing my balls like a Santa Claus sack around my head.
TOM: The sons of my sons will run in circles around me, each holding one of my ball sacs.
PETE: The sons of my sons will run around and around me until I am trapped in a prison of my own balls and flesh.
TOM: I will shout at them as they run away with my balls in their hands.
PETE: I will comfort you in your pain.

TOM: Deliver your heart unto my hand.
PETE: My shepherd will guide you in the field.
TOM: There will be no more cause for sorrow.
PETE: You will sleep with the lambs upon the earth.
TOM: Amen.

(Pause.
The chanting "hai" and "fai" are pronounced like the
word "hi.")

PETE: Hai, hai, a-shing-a-shing hai, a mekka-lek hai mekka
shing-a-shing fai.
TOM: Hai, hai, a-ding-a-ding hai, a wokka-wok hai mekka
fikky-fock fai.
PETE: Hai, hai, a-fing-a-fong hai, a wikka-wok hai mekka
ching-a-chong hai.
TOM: Hai, hai, a ching-a-ching hai, ma-lekka-lek hai donga
fing-a-fing hai.
PETE: Hai, hai, a-shing-a-shing hai, a likka-luk hai mekka
ching-a-ching fai.
TOM: Hai, hai, a-ding-a-dong hai, a likka-lik hai mekka
fikky-fock fai.
PETE: Hai, hai, a-fing-a-fong hai, a fikka-fock hai mekka
ching-a-chong hai.
TOM: Hai, hai, a ching-a-ching hai, ma-likka-lek hai donga
fikky-fock hai.

(Tom suddenly howls in pain.)

PETE: What's wrong?
TOM: I think I'm dying.
PETE: Why?
TOM: My eyes hurt.
PETE: You should get eye-removal surgery.
TOM: No!

(Pete howls in pain.)

What?
PETE *(Casually)*: Nothing.

(Tom howls in pain.)

Shut up, dude! You're not even hurt.
TOM: Yes I am.

(Pause.)

PETE: Help me.
TOM: You help me.
PETE: You help me first.
TOM: Some pretty sad things have happened to me. Do you
    want to hear about them?
PETE: Tell me about it tomorrow.
TOM: When I was five—
PETE: Do you know what's a good thing to do when you're sad?
TOM: Get drunk?
PETE: No.
TOM: Do cocaine?
PETE: No!
TOM: What then?
PETE: I don't know.
TOM: You're kind of an idiot.
PETE: You're an idiot! I know how to live!

(Tom howls in pain.)

TOM: Fuck!
PETE: Okay. I can help you.
TOM: How.
PETE: I can tell you how to live.
TOM: I already know how to live.

PETE: No, okay, this is it.

Do unto yourself as you would do unto another for whom you cared very deeply.

You have to be nice to yourself. For example, if your room is a total disaster area and you need to clean it but can't bring yourself to start doing it, just imagine that you're cleaning it for a really good friend who just found out they have cancer. But really, that friend is you.

(Tom is baffled.)

I'm trying to say that you should be motivated by compassion to yourself. Instead of telling yourself that you're a lazy slob for not cleaning your room, you should tell yourself that you deserve to have a clean room and that cleaning it is a nice thing to do for yourself.

TOM: That sounds like something for pussies.

PETE: See! That's the *opposite* of how to live! You think you can roll around in your sea of jelly balls like a big jelly whale, but eventually the jelly ball fluid is going to leak out and kill you!

(Tory leaves the giving up area and sings to Pete, calming him. A double "hh" at the end of a syllable indicates that a note is held for an extra beat.)

TORY:

Hikk-en yaa, chunken yaa, moo-oo-kohh-oh-ko chunyeh

PETE:

Hikk-en yaa, chunken yaa, moo-oo-kohh-oh-ko chunyeh

TORY:

Sayleh-kah-malikka-chah-mahah-maluk-alukohh-oh-ko chunyeh

PETE:

    Sayleh-kah-malikka-chah-hah. Maluk-ohh-oh-ko
    chunyeh

TORY:

    Hikk-en yaa, chunken yaa, moo-oo-kohh-oh-ko
    chunyeh

PETE:

    Hikk-en yaa, chunken yaa, moo-oo-kohh-oh-ko
    chunyeh

TORY *(Spoken)*: A-shee-shee.

PETE AND TORY *(Singing together)*:
    Sayleh-kah-malikka-chah-mahah-maluk-alukohh-
      oh-ko chunyeh
    Sayleh-kah-malikka-chah-hah. Maluk-ohh-oh-ko
    chunyeh.

TOM: This is a seminar on how to be cool.

TORY: I want to crack open a monkey's ribcage and dump a
pile of worms on top of its internal organs to see how they
all interact.

PETE: There are many ways of being cool.

TOM: I'm obsessed with things getting stuck into people's
eyeballs, like that precise moment of when the foreign
object pierces the jelly of the ball. I can imagine it over
and over again in my mind for hours. Like the idea of
being able to give someone a paper cut on both eyeballs
with one swipe.

TORY: What else is cool?

PETE: This sucks! I hate this!

(Pete exits.)

TORY: On my farm, there are some ducks.
TOM: I love all God's creation, to the smallest hair on their head.
TORY: Do you love my ducks?
TOM: I love all God's creation.
TORY: I love my ducks' duck meat.
TOM: I will protect their duck meat.
TORY: From what?

(Pause.)

TOM: Wolves.
TORY: There are no wolves on my farm.
TOM: You're going to hell.
TORY: Why?
TOM: Because you don't have Jesus in your heart.
TORY: How come?
TOM: Because you didn't invite him. It's like with vampires—
you have to invite him or he can't come in.
TORY: What happens if he comes in?
TOM: What do you want to happen?
TORY: I want to be a mermaid.
TOM: If you invite Jesus into your heart, then you can be a
mermaid.
TORY: How?
TOM: Because when you die you'll go to heaven, and heaven
is a mermaid fairyland.
TORY: Are you serious?
TOM: Absolutely.

*(Pause. Tory is overjoyed. She takes Tom's hand. Tom smiles
a big, forced smile.*
*They smile and hold hands. Tom's smile disintegrates
and he lets go of her hand.)*

TOM *(To the audience)*: I don't know how to live. I don't know
how to act around other people. I have no idea what the
fuck I'm doing.

And it scares me to look out there at you, because I'm afraid that you are all living your lives on instinct and feeling totally fine, while I'm all alone in my fucked-up state.

(To Tory) Sorry.

(Tom exits.
Pause.
Tory walks downstage, smiling at the audience.)

TORY: One summer, I drove across the country. I wasn't driving, so I actually ended up sleeping through a lot of it. It was ridiculous how much I slept. I think I slept like twelve hours a day for six days straight, which was weird because normally I'm not a big sleeper. I remember constantly half waking up to the feeling of the air conditioner combined with the feeling of heat pressing down on the outside of the car. The first thing that would register was the brightness through the windows, and then the radio. I could stay in that half awake state for a really long time, like an hour, without any kind of interruption. Whenever we stopped at gas stations I was usually half asleep and remember stumbling through the heat and then suddenly getting all alert when I got in the store and saw all this stuff I wanted to buy, like something to drink or a magazine or cassette tape. When we got back on the road I'd drink my drink and look at the different landscapes going past the windows.

I was surrounded by mermaids. I was lying on soft green grass and they were standing on their flippers in a circle around me. I looked up and saw a bright blue sky crisscrossed with rainbows that arched from one puffy white cloud to another. As I sat up, the mermaids started hopping away and I could see that the landscape around me was composed almost entirely of chopped-up mermaid parts.

There were mountains of mermaid–tail fish slices and mermaid torsos planted like bushes all around. Mermaid guts hung from all the trees and the lakes were clogged with mermaid hair. The fields were littered with squirming mermaid babies who lay unattended as hundreds of frolicking mermaids played kickball with hundreds of mermaid heads.

As I walked to my waiting rainbow coach, squashing a mermaid baby head with each step, I realized how fortunate I truly am.

END OF PLAY

The Appeal

For Linda Kuwatani

Production History

The Appeal was originally produced by Young Jean Lee's Theater Company. It premiered in April 2004 at Soho Rep in New York. It was directed by Young Jean Lee; the set and lighting design were by Eric Dyer, the costume design was by Tara Webb, original music was composed by Matmos and the sound design was by Yehuda Duenyas. It was performed by:

DOROTHY	Maggie Hoffman
WORDSWORTH	Pete Simpson
COLERIDGE	Michael Portnoy
BYRON	James Stanley

Characters

DOROTHY
WORDSWORTH
COLERIDGE
BYRON

Setting

1800. Dorothy and William Wordsworth's cottage in Grasmere. Every scene of Act One (including the fishing, gardening and hiking scenes) takes place in the same room, which
contains only a desk and chair. On the desk is a sheet of paper,
a feather, two books and an unlit candle in a holder.

Music

The electronic musicians Matmos composed original songs for
The Appeal, which are referred to in the stage directions. To
purchase the CD, you may contact info@youngjeanlee.org.

Act One

Scene 1

Lights down.
  Matmos's "Jig (Drunk)" begins.
  Lights fade up slowly on Wordsworth writing at his desk.
  Music fades out.
  Wordsworth stops writing.

WORDSWORTH: Ah, my poem is finished.

Scene 2

Wordsworth and Coleridge are fishing.

WORDSWORTH: What is a poet?
COLERIDGE: You and me are poets, Wordsworth, because we
    write poetry
WORDSWORTH: That's a simple answer, Coleridge.
COLERIDGE: What's the more sophisticated one.

WORDSWORTH: Well, I think a poet is someone who has more sensitivities than other people.

COLERIDGE: What sensitivities.

WORDSWORTH: Let me tell you what I mean. For example, a base ordinary man will look at a frog and just think "frog." With a poet, it's completely different. Do you know why? Because he is pleased and satisfied to contemplate the spirit of life which flows through himself, so that when he views the frog he sees his own inherent glories reflected in that animal. And then it gets even more sophisticated. Because say for example there is no frog. Then the poet can look at a frog in his imagination and see his glories reflected therein.

COLERIDGE: Why does he have to look at a frog?

WORDSWORTH: He doesn't.

COLERIDGE: Why can't he look at a chair.

WORDSWORTH: He can.

COLERIDGE: Well, if he can look at a chair then why does he have to pretend he's looking at a frog? Why doesn't he just look at whatever happens to be around him and see his glories reflected therein? It makes no sense.

WORDSWORTH: You didn't let me get to the even more sophisticated part.

COLERIDGE: How can I let you go on to the more sophisticated part when the first level of it makes no sense? You can't just layer one sophisticated thing on top of the other after another because you feel like it.

WORDSWORTH: I can't help it that you're too stupid to understand my concepts, Coleridge. If I made them less confusing then it wouldn't be the same ideas.

COLERIDGE: Okay, so what's the second level of sophistication?

WORDSWORTH: When we last left off, the poet was looking at the frog in his imagination and seeing his glories reflected therein. An ordinary base man also has the capability to look at a frog in his imagination, but he can't feel any passion about it because he isn't looking at a real frog,

110

whereas the poet can have a passion about the imaginary frog that is almost as good as the passion he would feel about the real frog. This makes him good at expressing what he thinks and feels.

COLERIDGE: I don't want to talk about this anymore.

WORDSWORTH: Okay.

COLERIDGE: I want to talk about something I'm interested in, which is what's the difference between fancy and the imagination.

WORDSWORTH: Okay.

COLERIDGE: Average people like you think that "fancy" and "imagination" are synonyms for the same thing, or that they represent the high and low ends of one concept. But no. They are two distinct things. I can't think of anything that is less like the Greek word "phantasia" than the Latin word "imaginatio," but in society there is a secret shared impulse to make things better, and so that impulse has been trying to make the two words "fancy" and "imagination" be more different. A bunch of dialects supplied them to the more homogenous languages like Greek and German, and also the same things happened in mixed languages like ours for the same reason, but also because of accidents of translation from original works of different countries.

WORDSWORTH: I can't understand anything you're saying.

COLERIDGE: Okay, dummy. All I'm saying is that "fancy" and "imagination" started out being the same thing, but that society, which is always moving towards the better, has been stretching them apart to make them different over the years.

WORDSWORTH: Why do you say it in a confusing way?

COLERIDGE: It's not confusing—you're just stupid.

WORDSWORTH: You're stupid! You couldn't understand anything I was saying.

COLERIDGE: You couldn't understand anything I was saying.

Scene 3

Dorothy is gardening and writing in her journal.
Wordsworth enters.

DOROTHY: Hi Wordsworth.
WORDSWORTH: Hi Dorothy my sister.
DOROTHY: Will you hoe the beets.
WORDSWORTH: Okay.

(Wordsworth hoes beets.
Coleridge enters, whistling.)

Aah, the birds of the field, toil not nor labor do they spin.
DOROTHY: Hi Coleridge.
COLERIDGE: Hi Dorothy, hi Wordsworth.
WORDSWORTH: Hi Coleridge.
    I don't know what, but I think that nature is making me have a nature inside that writes poetry. Uhh . . . oh, I remember. So I take one look at these refreshing beets and the good ones start pouring out of me in measured strain and it made me like a holy priest, blessed for the day. And then, uhh . . . everyone will remember it because I wroted it down. And then, uhh . . . oh yeah that thing inside me again, but I don't remember what it did. Uhhh . . . oh yeah that's right my voice was saying stuff and then there was an inside voice that was better and it echoed the outside, inferior voice and I liked how it sounds. Listen to my theory. There is an outside one and an inside one, and they match. It makes sense.
COLERIDGE: What are you talking about.
WORDSWORTH: Okay, dummy. If I look at these beets, they look refreshing, right?
COLERIDGE: So?
WORDSWORTH: So, the beets are the outside thing, and my

genius to write poems is the inside thing, and then it's like a call-and-response, where the beets look refreshing and then my genius comes out and writes a poem.

(Pause.)

COLERIDGE: Do you want to hear my new poem.

DOROTHY: Oh, yes.

COLERIDGE: Once upon a time I went to a wedding. I was normal, but the crazy man jumps to me and goes, "Bla bla bla," until I threatened to staff him one. The crazy one said, *(Gruff voice)* "I want to tell you," *(Normal voice)* and I said, "Tell me some fun ones," but he hypnotized me and I fell down.

So the old man said, *(Gruff voice)* "The ship goed away all happy, and then the sun goed up and then the sun goed down and then the sun goed up and then the sun goed down." *(Normal voice)* At this point I beat my chest because I heard the bassoon and remembered about the fun ones, but what can I do?

And then the crazy guy says, *(Gruff voice)* "What happens is that it rains and goes crazy, and then the 'nother ones and 'nother ones come all ice and cracking noises, and then there is a bird. We call the bird by its name, "Hi, Chico," and then gived it worms from the cookie-biscuits, so then the ice makes a big crack from the thunderstorm, and we goed through it."

(Normal voice) Then I said, "Why are you going so crazy?" and he said, *(Gruff voice)* "I shooted it that bird with my crossbow."

Then—

WORDSWORTH: So then the ancient mariner said, *(Gruff voice)* "Yar! Ahoy! I wanted to take a break from me poetry, so I goes to a green place and sits and looks around, and there is the sun going this way and that way.

So then I think, should I choose this way or that way to go? And then I look into my mind's eye, and there is a cottage that my fancy paints pictureful."

COLERIDGE: You ruined my poem, Wordsworth.

WORDSWORTH: So.

COLERIDGE: I don't like it.

(Pause.)

DOROTHY: I have a story. It's about what I did yesterday and the day before yesterday. The day before yesterday the weather was this way and that way, and then the rain didn't let me go for a walk. The next day the weather was warm and mild, so I walked to Pokey's house with an armload of books and gathered some soft plants along the way. Then I wished I had a botany book so that I could list all the different ones I saw. I saw a red flower and a blue flower and a green flower. And then I went round by the stepping stones, and the weather was this way and that way.

WORDSWORTH: That's not a story it's a description.

Scene 4

Matmos's "Emmy (Full)" starts.

Wordsworth, Coleridge and Dorothy hike around the stage with walking sticks, jumping over an imaginary stream, looking out into the horizon, crawling under the desk, etc.

Wordsworth and Coleridge are completely absorbed in each other.

Wordsworth helps Coleridge jump over a "stream" and they high-five each other, while Dorothy struggles over alone.

The Appeal

Scene 5

Wordsworth, Coleridge and Dorothy are having tea.

COLERIDGE: When it is three people speaking, it is hard because it doesn't just go back and forth.

DOROTHY: We can't even differentiate from between us, except for Wordsworth is obsessed with nature and has an abnormal name.

COLERIDGE: But the real question is: why are we having tea?

WORDSWORTH: I haven't spoken for a while.

DOROTHY: Go on.

WORDSWORTH: Shut up! I'm going to try to muster a long speech, here. Okay. Okay. So the tea could be symbolic.

(Pause.)

DOROTHY: It's not a long speech if you just stop.

WORDSWORTH: It would be a long speech if you would quit interrupting me.

COLERIDGE: Yeah!

WORDSWORTH: Okay, so here's the thing. I'm too mortified by all of this to even continue. I don't even know if I can make a long speech because my motivation is so stupid.

COLERIDGE: Isn't that a form of laziness, to say that everything you do is so stupid? It's like covering your bases so that you can never be accused of being deluded, but it's lazy thinking because you never have to separate the wheat from the chaff.

(Pause.)

DOROTHY: I can't believe how slowly it all goes.

COLERIDGE: Shouldn't there be a story?

WORDSWORTH: What, you mean like one that you make up?

COLERIDGE: Yeah, I guess so. A made-up story.

WORDSWORTH: I can't, because my heart is broken.

DOROTHY: Why is your heart broken?

COLERIDGE: That's a dead end. It looks as though I'm going to have to step in. Here's what we'll do. First, we'll remark upon the tea, each with our own distinct personality. Since I am already starting to be practical and businesslike, I will begin, and even attempt to incorporate a story, which is the hardest thing of all.

(Pause.)

The water is rising, but we are safe in this garden. Let's build a raft so that when the water is at a more safer level, then we can row out and attempt to save our lives.

DOROTHY: How nice to have a leader to follow!

COLERIDGE: Shut up! You're ruining it!

DOROTHY: Oh, sorry.

But I'm too scared to go out on the water.

COLERIDGE: There is nothing to fear but fear itself.

DOROTHY: Now you're ruining it!

WORDSWORTH: Why can't anything ever just work out? You start trying to do something well and then it just fucks up.

DOROTHY: We could remark upon the physical properties of the sandwiches.

COLERIDGE: The question that haunts me is what's going to happen next. Because there's always something that you have to do to fix things.

WORDSWORTH: Not always.

COLERIDGE: What are you talking about, Wordsworth? Do you even know which words are coming out of your mouth?

WORDSWORTH: This is straightforward and not oblique. What could be more shameful?

COLERIDGE: Shame! This is shameful!

DOROTHY: Oh, shame, shame.

COLERIDGE: Good! We're building up a kind of chorus of intertwining words. It's very, very good and I like it.

WORDSWORTH: It's taking too long! I want to shut out the light!

DOROTHY: It's almost here!

COLERIDGE: We still have a little ways to go.

WORDSWORTH: Should we make any of the traditional gestures?

COLERIDGE *(To Dorothy)*: Hey, Honora!

DOROTHY: What?

COLERIDGE: Your name just changed.

DOROTHY: It did? To what?

COLERIDGE: To Honus. *(Pronounced "Hoe-nuss")*

Scene 6

Wordsworth, Coleridge and Dorothy are having tea.

Matmos's "Jig (Rock)" starts.

Coleridge puts opium in their tea and they drink it.

They start hallucinating and Dorothy and Coleridge stagger to different corners of the room.

Wordsworth takes off his shirt and lies on his back on top of the desk, knocking things on the floor. He sticks his hand down his pants.

They all masturbate furiously. Dorothy spanks herself with her diary.

Lights out.

Scene 7

In the darkness.

WORDSWORTH *(Reciting)*:

> And before hell mouth; dry plain and two mountains;
> On the one mountain, a running form, and another
> In the turn of the hill; in hard steel

The road like a slow screw's thread,
The angle almost imperceptible, so that the circuit
    seemed hardly to rise;
And the running form, naked, Blake,
Shouting, whirling his arms, the swift limbs,
Howling against the evil, his eyes rolling,
Whirling like flaming cart-wheels, and his head
    held backward to gaze on the evil
As he ran from it, to be hid by the steel mountain,
And when he showed again from the north side; his
    eyes blazing toward hell mouth,
His neck forward, and like him Peire Cardinal.
And in the west mountain, Il Fiorentino,
Seeing hell in his mirror, and lo Sordels
Looking on it in his shield;
And Augustine, gazing toward the invisible.

Scene 8

Lights up.
    The room is in disarray.
    Dorothy and Wordsworth are badly hungover.

DOROTHY: You're a total and complete fucking moron.
WORDSWORTH: What?
DOROTHY: What.
WORDSWORTH: You just said that I was a total and complete
    fucking moron.
DOROTHY: Oh. I was talking to myself.
WORDSWORTH: Oh.

(Pause.)

Why don't we have any fucking medicine?

DOROTHY: I wish someone would come and just take me away from here.

WORDSWORTH: Where is the medicine, Dorothy.

DOROTHY: The frogs.

WORDSWORTH: Dorothy.

DOROTHY: The frogs!

WORDSWORTH: My head.

DOROTHY: Five pigs.

WORDSWORTH: I thought there was medicine.

DOROTHY: Two fish. One dog.

WORDSWORTH: Be quiet Dorothy.

DOROTHY: There's a rat somewhere and the animals keep coming.

WORDSWORTH: It makes my head hurt.

DOROTHY: The animals keep coming at me.

WORDSWORTH *(Groaning)*: Ooh.

DOROTHY: Five bears go into a house. The first bear says, "Where's my mom?" and the second bear says, "Fuck you, you don't need any mom," and the other one says, "This is all meaningless. I want some meaning."

WORDSWORTH: That's really awful Dorothy.

DOROTHY: There is no monkey.

WORDSWORTH: Shut up shut up.

DOROTHY: How many buffalo do you have? Why are there so many animals? I don't know where the elephants are!

(Wordsworth groans.)

Here's the thing. Can you forget the past and the future and concentrate on the present, which feels like a blinding white light. The blinding white light tries to wipe everything out but it can't. It just keeps you awake in the early morning hours while you have a headache and are trying not to remember things. But your mind keeps strategizing and you can't fall back asleep.

WORDSWORTH: What does that have to do with Coleridge.

DOROTHY: I'm getting to that. When you have a headache, you can't block out the past and the future in a blinding white light, because once you get inside the blinding white light what you have is present physical sensation, and if you're unhealthy or sick or a drunk like me then you have this weird feeling that is bad. And so all that work blocking out the past and the future goes to nothing, because the most presentest of present moments feels like complete and total shit. And it doesn't matter because the memories of past humiliations always creep in anyway.

WORDSWORTH: There's a clog somewhere.

DOROTHY: No there isn't.

WORDSWORTH: Before I knew what to do, but now there's a clog.

DOROTHY: What clog.

WORDSWORTH: I want access to the good stuff, but I don't know if I'm getting it or not. I feel like I might not be getting access to the good stuff, but I have no way of knowing. What I want to know is how does one get access to the good stuff.

DOROTHY: It's very simple, dummy. If you try to think of something off the top of your head that comes from deep within your psyche, what you get is animals. Chickens and monkeys and cows and stuff. It's true. Why are animals coming out? Who knows.

WORDSWORTH: Maybe it's just you.

DOROTHY: Huh?

WORDSWORTH: Maybe it's just you that has animals in your psyche.

DOROTHY: No, it's everyone.

(Long pause.)

I hate you!

WORDSWORTH: You hate me?

DOROTHY: No, I was saying it to myself.

Scene 9

Wordsworth puts the room in order.
He sits down at his desk and writes.

WORDSWORTH *(Putting down his pen)*: Ah, my poem is finished.

> *(To the audience)* Hi, my name is William Wordsworth. You might have heard of me. I'm one of the poets known as English Romantic. Other Romantic poets include: Blake, Coleridge, Byron, Shelley, and Keats. We all existed in the nineteenth century. I'll tell you a little more about us later, but right now I'm going to tell the story of my life.

(Pause.)

> Oh, but I have a problem. Not the sky, nor the birds, nor the bush, nor the breeze can erase this problem that I have, and who knows if it will be fixed or not. That is the question. Will the problem be fixed, or will the problem not be fixed? Here is the problem. Coleridge and I are in a fight. Stay tuned for further details.

(Dorothy enters.)

DOROTHY: Hi Wordsworth.
WORDSWORTH: Hi Dorothy my sister.
DOROTHY: Wordsworth, are you and Coleridge still in a fight?
WORDSWORTH: Yes, Dorothy.
DOROTHY: Will the problem be fixed, or will it not be fixed?
WORDSWORTH: I don't know, my sister.
DOROTHY: Well, Coleridge is outside right now, so why don't we bring him inside and then you two can make up?

WORDSWORTH: Okay.

(Dorothy exits.)

(To the audience) Let me tell you some more about the English Romantic poets. Blake was the first one, and some people say that he doesn't count because he was something else, but I think he counts because I don't know. Here is what Blake was like.

(Coleridge enters as Blake with furious expression on his face, whirling his arms like windmills.)

One time, Blake and I met each other.

(Wordsworth goes over to Blake.)

Hi, Blake.

(Blake ignores him, whirls arms, etc.)

What's the matter with you?

(Blake ignores him, whirls arms, etc.)

You're too crazy for me. I don't care about your poetry.

*(Wordsworth pushes Blake offstage.
Dorothy enters with Coleridge.)*

DOROTHY: Here's Coleridge.
WORDSWORTH: Hi Coleridge.
COLERIDGE: I'm mad at you Wordsworth.
WORDSWORTH: Why?
COLERIDGE: I'm not going to say.
WORDSWORTH: Can't we make up now?
COLERIDGE: No.

WORDSWORTH: Let's make up Coleridge.

COLERIDGE: No I won't.

DOROTHY: I have some things I have to do in the other room.

(Dorothy exits.)

WORDSWORTH: Coleridge, are we not fellow brothers?

COLERIDGE: We're not brothers.

WORDSWORTH: Oh Coleridge, does not our brothership go far deeper than mere flesh and bone?

COLERIDGE: How?

WORDSWORTH: We are poet-brothers, my dear Coleridge, and this bond can never be displaced, because it is a brothership of my spirit.

COLERIDGE: So what.

WORDSWORTH: Oh Coleridge, how can you be so blind. Do you not know what it means to be a true poet?

COLERIDGE: Of course I know.

WORDSWORTH: Sometimes I wonder if you do.

COLERIDGE: That's an insult!

(Coleridge knocks everything off the desk. He exits.)

WORDSWORTH *(To the audience)*: Oh no. I was trying to make things better with Coleridge, but I only made them worse.

(Dorothy enters.)

DOROTHY: What happened.

WORDSWORTH: I was trying to make things better with Coleridge, but I only made them worse.

DOROTHY: Maybe it will help if I talk to him.

WORDSWORTH: The suspense is too much for me, Dorothy. Will the problem be fixed, or will it not be fixed? Will we ever be able to find out why Coleridge is mad?

DOROTHY: Don't worry, Wordsworth. I'll go talk to him.

(Dorothy exits.)

WORDSWORTH *(To the audience)*: Oops, I almost forgot to tell
you about Byron. He was considered as a rock musician
in our time. Once I met him at a big party in London.

(Coleridge enters as Byron, holding a glass of champagne.)

Hi Byron.
BYRON: Who are you?
WORDSWORTH: I'm Wordsworth.
BYRON: I know you. You're the one who wrote those namby-
pamby poems.
    What are you staring at, you stinking tax-collector?
WORDSWORTH: I can't help being a tax-collector. I have to
support my family.
BYRON: You must be pretty shocked to meet someone who
tells things like it is. I have another shocking one, too.
You've never heard any news like this before. The prime
minister, Spencer Perceval, has just been assassinated in
the House of Commons.

(Wordsworth is very shocked.
  Byron exits.)

WORDSWORTH: That's when I knew that I was really in the
toast of things.

Scene 10

Coleridge and Dorothy are standing together.
  *Wordsworth enters with Coleridge's suitcases, throws them
on the floor, and sits behind his desk.*
  Coleridge picks up his bags.

DOROTHY: Good-bye, Coleridge.
COLERIDGE: Good-bye, Dorothy.

(Coleridge bangs Wordsworth's chair with his suitcase as he passes it.)

Good-bye, Wordsworth.
WORDSWORTH: Bye-bye, Fuckface!

(Coleridge exits.
Dorothy goes over to Wordsworth.)

DOROTHY: Are you all right?
WORDSWORTH: Yes.
DOROTHY: Do you want to go for a walk?
WORDSWORTH: No.
　　　　I wasn't an asshole, was I?
　　　　Was I an asshole?
DOROTHY: No . . .
WORDSWORTH: I was trying to be really nice to him.
DOROTHY: I know. You were trying to be really nice.
WORDSWORTH: But I feel bad.
DOROTHY: Listen.
　　　　The title of the song we're listening to is "Allegra Dolce Amore Conquista." Mozart scratched all these songs on a stone wall when he was in a mental institution, and from the outside, from this cold clinical pristine place of distance, where it's just this cold image in your mind, it seems beautiful. But in reality, the way it felt, I don't know, maybe it was beautiful then as well. Maybe the people who look so beautiful from the outside, like they're propelled by this force of nature, this weird animalistic mindless energy, maybe that feels like nothing. Maybe it feels like air, like time passing without knowing it, like empty time, like empty time with . . . that is full—that is empty of your mind and ego and full of expe-

rience, of moment to moment experience of the physical, of the—things come in, images and events and people and whatever, and they just go in and there is no filter, there is no self-consciousness.

Your life will be filled with laughter and beauty, and it will be at the expense of whatever idiots and victims may fall on your path.

(Lights out.
    Matmos's "In a Ring" plays during transition to Act Two.)

Act Two

Scene 1

A month later. Byron's castle in the Higher Alps and its environs, represented by a room containing only a red velvet sofa with two books at its feet.

Wordsworth, Dorothy and Byron are eating dessert.

Byron is much more formally dressed than Wordsworth and Dorothy. He wears a ridiculously high, stiff collar.

BYRON: I can't go crazy with the storage and the cheapness—it has to be attractive. Does it have to be natural wood to look good, or can it be birch? The natural wood shelves are cheapest, but the natural wood furniture is more expensive. Don't they have to match? I could get birch furniture and match it with birch shelves—maybe that would be cheaper because shelves are cheaper than furniture. But then again maybe I need a lot of shelves. For the desk I can use the big desk, the little sofa table, or the unfinished wood table. For the dining table I can use the little sofa table, the unfinished wood table, or the glazed wood table. The sofa table may be too small and too low, and the big desk may be too ugly. If I got the natural tables then they would be pretty big but then they could match with natural wood shelves. But wouldn't fake birch look better with the metal stuff I'm getting for sure?

(Wordsworth stands up abruptly.)

WORDSWORTH *(Shouting)*: You only want to talk about furniture!

BYRON: So.

DOROTHY: Oh Byron, you invited Wordsworth and me here to your castle in the Alps.

Scene 2

Byron and Wordsworth are sitting together. Byron looks uncomfortable.

WORDSWORTH: I have this idea in my head of a person who is like a membrane filled with stuff, and the membrane is all self-contained and okay and the person doesn't humiliate themselves. But with me it's the opposite. I can't seem to control my mouth or body or anything, and something that I'm doing is always slightly wrong. I don't know how to define it.

BYRON: Oh.

WORDSWORTH: I constantly make these ejaculations of noise.

BYRON: Ah.

WORDSWORTH: It's when you remember a humiliation and then say something like "I hate you" or repeat fragments of a conversation in your head. It's an instinctive response and I've started to do it even in public.

BYRON: Oh?

WORDSWORTH: Everything sucks!
BYRON: Ah . . .
WORDSWORTH: Everything!
BYRON: Oh.

(Byron surreptitiously picks up a book and starts looking at it.)

WORDSWORTH: Because I'm horribly, terribly sick. Do you know how you can have some kind of emotional problem and everything seems awful? But then you get a physical problem and you remember how good it is when you don't have a physical problem and how easy everything should be as long as you don't have a physical problem.
BYRON *(Looking through the book)*: Ah.
WORDSWORTH: Why can't you feel your own luck? When people are beggars and sleeping on church lawns, why can't you appreciate what you have and stop feeling so sorry for yourself and so horrible, like life is a nightmare? I wonder if other people ever get that feeling—that life is a nightmare and it won't end. That something is weird and wrong and immoral and sinister, and that concrete things don't exist.

(Pause.)

BYRON: I think that Shakespeare was in my house.

Scene 3

Matmos's "Jig (Full)" starts.
    Dorothy enters on one side of the stage and Byron leaps onstage from the other side.
    Byron does a fancy jig all around the room while Dorothy watches.

Byron starts dancing with Dorothy, abandons her in a frenzy of solo dance, and then awkwardly grabs her in an amorous embrace.

Scene 4

Dorothy and Byron are drinking.
Dorothy is looking adoringly at Byron, while Byron looks detached.

DOROTHY: I don't know how to feel anymore.
　　　That was not a true statement. That just popped out of my subconscious.
BYRON: Have you been enjoying your stay here, Dorothy?
DOROTHY: Oh Byron, this morning I went into a room that had flayed fox and badger pelts all spread out hanging in glass cases and nobody was in the room, and it was horrible.

(Pause.)

Oh Byron, will you recite one of your poems to me?
BYRON: Uh, sure.

　　　Ching Chong Chinaman
　　　Chinkety-Ching
　　　Wing Wong Wang Wung
　　　Bing Bang Bing

　　　Ching Chong Chinaman
　　　Chinkety-Chang
　　　Bing Bong Bang Bung
　　　Wing Wong Wang.

DOROTHY: Oh.
BYRON: What's wrong Dorothy.

DOROTHY: It's just this fear, this horrible fear, of having something lovely and dreamed-of and hoped-for snatched away from me because of this veil of illusion striped over my eyes.

BYRON: What?

Scene 5

Wordsworth, Dorothy and Byron are having tea.
Wordsworth cries out in anguish.
Byron tries to caress Dorothy's arm but she slaps his hand away.
Dorothy is wearing a big fur muff, and throughout the scene she squirms her hands around in the muff and sucks her teeth loudly.
Byron is weirded-out by them.

WORDSWORTH: I wish I could capture the essence of this messiness. Clean is when you get up in the morning and do things that you need to do and comport yourself in a natural and blameless manner. I feel that the rest of the world operates this way, although I know that many people have problems with motivation. But the natural and blameless manner seems rampant among anyone whom I admire.

BYRON: The distinction is not clear to me between the blameless manner and the blameful one.

WORDSWORTH: It's bad. It's very, very bad.

Then there is the saddest thing of all, which is the horrible sadness from knowing that I will not be hanging out with Coleridge tonight and getting all of the wonderful things that came to me last month when he was visiting.

BYRON: There is no reason why you shouldn't feel better.

WORDSWORTH: Yes, I am sick. Yes, I cannot speak. But I am lucky, lucky, lucky, and everyone knows and hates me for it.

I feel like a boil, a blot on the face of the Earth. This is the way that rich people feel sometimes, and they are the lowest of the low.

BYRON *(Offended)*: Maybe you are talking to the wrong person. I no longer have any kind of good sense for things.

WORDSWORTH: I'm sick.

When you're sick, you remember how much better it was to be well, but when you're well, you're so crippled by mental anguish that you feel sick, even though it's not the same thing at all. The horror is when people get sick and stay that way all the time, or when you discover five small round bald spots on your head and nobody can explain why. But here's an interesting question: is the mental anguish that comes from cosmetic aberration the equivalent of the physical pain that comes from being really sick?

There are always shades upon shades, and I'm sick of it.

BYRON: That's nothing.

WORDSWORTH: What is?

BYRON: Your problems. My problem is much bigger.

WORDSWORTH: What is it?

BYRON: I have an anxiety.

WORDSWORTH: What anxiety.

(Pause.)

BYRON: I'm afraid of what it would be like if I had microscopes for eyes.

WORDSWORTH: That will never happen.

BYRON: Don't you see why it would be such a terror to have microscopes for eyes?

WORDSWORTH: I guess so, but it will never happen.

BYRON: The fact that one can even think it—it creates a horrifying sense of possibility.

Scene 6

Dorothy is lying with her head in Byron's lap. They are both drunk and continue to drink throughout the scene.

BYRON: This is my secret place that I go to when I need to be alone. A cottage among the Bernese Alps.
DOROTHY: Ooh.

(Pause.)

BYRON: Have you ever had a cold, drunk alcohol on top of that cold, and then woken up the next morning?
DOROTHY: I'm not much of a drinker.
BYRON: It gives you a weird feeling.
DOROTHY: That's why I don't drink.
BYRON: It doesn't let you access things.
DOROTHY: Try.
BYRON: Okay, faces blowing up in the moonlight. Chickens crowing to kingdom come please mother won't you give me some camphor, bicarbonate of soda whatever, I can't seem to stop myself. Angels hovering in the midair with their middies drawn tight about their supple waists and this is bullshit bullshit bullshit and I can't seem to stop myself I can't seem to stop when will this end? What is this bullshit these explosions these implosions of sound where you remember past humiliations and explode. Past humiliations including engaging in physical things with someone and then putting your foot on their chair in a proprietary way and then having them avoid you and ignore you and not respond to any of your attempts to solicit a response.
DOROTHY: Oh Byron.
BYRON: This is what I want I want cleanliness and purity and everything to be in order and for my personality to stay within certain outlines certain parameters certain out-

lines a shape of what a person is supposed to be is supposed to be without humiliating themselves or sending
out tentacles of dirtiness into the world where things
become contaminated by their desire, their weakness,
their selfishness, their greed, all of the things that make
them despicable and make them want to shout out their
own inadequacies into the stillness of the expensive
loaned-out castle with the swanky neighbors who have
their secrets their threatening secrets that may not be
very good secrets at all but rather something that makes
you feel dull.

DOROTHY: Oh Byron you sound like Wordsworth.

Scene 7

Coleridge's head appears above the back wall of the set.

COLERIDGE: Nobody understands the torture and the misery.
Why is this happening to me? Why has it never been this
bad before? I want to kill myself now more than ever.

The misery and the torture, the torture and the misery.
Why is this happening to me? Okay, let me think of a catalog of my miseries. There are too many, they are all
pressing against the inside of my head like a poison
cloud of horror. How many things are hurting me, pressing me? How many things are going to kill me? Now
I want to kill myself because . . .

Because I'm thinking I'm thinking because I don't
know my mind is a blank because because because
because because this language sounds horrible and good
speaking requires thought, some kind of gelling or mat-
uration process in the head that makes it filter through
the intelligence instead of . . .

Why do I want to kill myself?

I want to kill myself because I feel that I had finally, for the first time in my life, pumped my ego up close to the point where I had always dreamed of pumping it, like a kind of pinnacle of ego-pumpedness that reaches/touches close to my soul in a way that it never had before because I was doing things that were far away from my intents and degrees.

Let me list all the ways. Let me list all the wonderful, precious moments. There were all of the moments in which Dorothy expressed her attraction to me and flirted with me. There was the moment when Wordsworth hit my leg and then told me to sue him. There was the moment when Dorothy and Wordsworth invited me to come to Grasmere. There was the moment when Wordsworth smiled at me in the garden as if he were really glad to see me and liked me, and all of the subsequent smiles that looked like that, like the second day I was there, the day after I flirted with Dorothy in the hills, or some other day like Thursday after I'd flirted with her the week before, I think.

That is the painful thing.

Scene 8

Wordsworth and Dorothy are drinking and laughing. Byron sits apart from them, looking left out and miserable.

WORDSWORTH *(To Dorothy)*: What about the allies?
DOROTHY: Oh, ha ha!
WORDSWORTH: Are they allies or enemies?

*(Dorothy and Wordsworth laugh.
Coleridge enters, drinking.)*

DOROTHY: Le bel esprit comme on sait fut de tout temps l'ennemi le plus perfide du génie.

(Dorothy and Coleridge clink glasses.)

WORDSWORTH: Oh, Dorothy! Which reminds me, I found this in the gutter today.

(He takes a folded scrap of paper out of his pocket and reads:)

"The following letter hath laid before me many great and manifest evils in the world of letters which I had overlooked; but they open to me a very busy scene, and it will require no small care and application to amend errors which are become so universal."

I just find it so interesting, this idea of letters.

COLERIDGE: Yeah, letters.

DOROTHY: Letters are interesting.

WORDSWORTH: "World of letters." Does that sound weird to you? Or am I just being retarded.

COLERIDGE: I don't think you're being retarded. I think it's a strange wording.

DOROTHY: "World of letters." Yeah, I guess that's kind of weird.

WORDSWORTH: Also "a very busy scene." I kind of like that. It reminds me of that poem—do you remember the one?—in which all of the people are running around.

DOROTHY: No, I don't remember.

COLERIDGE: Yeah, me neither.

WORDSWORTH: Oh well.

I guess I'll stop boring you now.

(Everyone except Byron laughs.)

COLERIDGE: Hey, I wonder if there's any after-dinner sherry.

(Pause while everyone looks at Byron, who refuses to look at anyone.)

DOROTHY: Hey Byron, Coleridge just asked if there's sherry.

(Byron abruptly gets up and leaves the room.)

WORDSWORTH: Hm.
DOROTHY: I guess there's no sherry.
COLERIDGE: That's okay. I'm starting to get drunk anyway.

(Everyone laughs.)

Which reminds me, has anyone read anything good lately?
DOROTHY: Wordsworth and I have been rereading Virgil's
    Eclogues.
WORDSWORTH: Those Eclogues really piss me off.
DOROTHY: Oh Wordsworth.
WORDSWORTH: The only reason Corydon wins in Eclogue 7
    is that someone has to win for the purposes of dramatic
    smoothery. What kind of bullshit is that.
COLERIDGE: No, he's right. Because of that dead-heat in
    Eclogue 3, Corydon has to win in Eclogue 7.
DOROTHY: The thing that makes labor stuff valuable is how
    much . . . uh . . . how much you value that other stuff,
    which is something about necessity. Let's talk about that.

(Pause.)

WORDSWORTH: Or, to put it another way, "Wordsworth is
    right."

(Everyone laughs.)

Scene 9

BYRON: Oh boy. The pain is so bad I don't even know if I can
    speak.

So you get this feeling that the cycle of the past is going to repeat itself over and over, and you can never believe that it is happening again.

All I want to do is go into the other room and reach out and be reached by a human being. But I can't. And all the while my mind is calculating, calculating, to use this for material, and already the burden is lifting.

Is this . . . I can't say such a stupid thing. This is what happened . . . there are too many things that happened. What am I feeling right now? I am panicking because I am afraid that Wordsworth thinks that I am a psychopath asshole loser undesirable person and that everyone is talking about me behind my back and that I am going to be told that my presence is no longer desired. I am afraid that Wordsworth is talking to everyone behind my back saying that I am too unstable. I want to talk to him so badly and be reassured, but if I go back into the dining room then he will avoid me and I will not say a word but he will see that I am there and it will enhance this idea that I am a stalker. But if that's what he's already thinking then why not go on? What more damage could I do? Perhaps this will be the thing that drives me over the edge in his mind as someone who is crazy, and right now he has a lesser idea of my craziness.

There is this panic, this incredibly intense panic that you've lost everything. That you've lost everything through your complete inability to understand what you must do.

It's my house, so maybe I can go back in there. Are they talking about poetry right now? What the fuck is going on? Did they find the sherry? Will it be weird if I go back in there? I just want to go back in there.

(Pause.)

I just want to go back in there.

Scene 10

Wordsworth, Dorothy and Coleridge are still drinking.

COLERIDGE: There are still things that we need, like another process that pushes things down after things become hard, and in the case of the first pushdown, which is the second case, that the pushing happens one time and then another time.

WORDSWORTH: Oh no Dorothy, look what we've started!

(Everyone laughs.
Byron enters very suddenly and just stands there.
Everyone ignores him.)

DOROTHY: The plant brain is capable only of an idée fixe, which is why I'm more interested in plant feelings.

COLERIDGE: Are you calling me a vegetable, Dorothy?

(Coleridge tickles Dorothy, who squeals and tickles him back.)

DOROTHY *(Pulling away)*: Oh, oh! I almost forgot! I have a surprise!

(Dorothy exits.)

WORDSWORTH: Hello there, Byron.

BYRON: Hello.

WORDSWORTH: Would you like some sherry?

BYRON: All right.

(Byron pours sherry.)

COLERIDGE: Don't drink it all! I plan on having a second glass.

(Byron stops pouring.
   Coleridge takes the bottle and fills his own glass to the brim.)

WORDSWORTH: Why don't you have a seat?
BYRON: All right.

(He sits.)

COLERIDGE: Cigar?
BYRON: All right.

(Coleridge opens a cigar box and hands Byron a cigar, taking out two more for Wordsworth and himself. He lights all three.)

WORDSWORTH *(Smoking contentedly)*: Aah . . . Coleridge, do you remember that 1881 La Flor de La Isabela Robusto we shared on the boat in Spain?
COLERIDGE: As I recall, it was a bit dry on the finish.
WORDSWORTH: No, that was the Corona. The Robusto had bite.
COLERIDGE: Oh, that's right. It had a *little* bite.
WORDSWORTH: It was like the future of England, Coleridge, which is so glorious and will only become more so.

(Pause.)

So Byron, Dorothy tells me that you're writing a poem that makes fun of everything and everyone.
BYRON: I—I suppose so.
WORDSWORTH: Well, you seem like a fairly satirical type of person.
   I'm not being too . . . personal, am I?
BYRON *(Nervously puffing on his cigar)*: Come to think of it, I think I've had the 1881 La Flor de La Isabela before.

(He clears his throat.)

Wordsworth, I heard you're working on a new poem as well.

WORDSWORTH: Why, yes, I am.

COLERIDGE *(Getting up)*: Do you mind if I get the port from the other room?

BYRON: Oh, sure.

(Coleridge exits.)

I . . . I think your poems are so wonderful, Wordsworth.

WORDSWORTH: What? You do?

BYRON: I've read every one of them.

WORDSWORTH: You have? How?

BYRON: I just did.

WORDSWORTH: Well. I had no idea.

BYRON: I like "Yarrow Revisited" and "Most Sweet It Is with Unuplifted Eyes."

WORDSWORTH: You've read those?

BYRON: My favorite part of "Yarrow Revisited" is when it goes, "Brisk Youth appeared, the Morn of youth."

WORDSWORTH: Well! How about that?

BYRON: Do you know, Wordsworth, the critics say that in twenty years I will be the least honored and the most ignored and deplored out of all of us.

WORDSWORTH: Do you know what your problem is, Byron? You need to be more confident in yourself. You've got a wisecrack answer for everything. I admire that.

BYRON: You do?

WORDSWORTH: I sure do.

BYRON: Wow.

WORDSWORTH: It's too bad you're not as good at writing poetry as me and Coleridge.

(Dorothy and Coleridge enter laughing.

Dorothy is holding a pie and Coleridge is holding a bottle of port.)

DOROTHY: Look! I made a pie!
COLERIDGE: I found the port!

(The lights go out.)

WORDSWORTH, COLERIDGE AND DOROTHY: Ooh!
COLERIDGE: I saw some more candles in the gallery.
DOROTHY: I'll come with you, Coleridge.
WORDSWORTH: Ooh, what fun!

(Wordsworth, Coleridge and Dorothy exit.)

BYRON: Here's a candle.

(Byron lights a candle.
  His high, stiff collar casts an enormous shadow on the wall.)

There is something about procrastinating. About having a deadline and not doing anything until the deadline is almost past and then having the deadline pass. It is a nightmarish, horrible feeling. There is this part of it where you think that if you had only started the moment the project began, how much easier and more lovely and wonderful everything would have been. Then there is this horrible, nightmarish sensation that comes when you realize how much you have to do and how all of the time you had to do it in has been squandered by you yet again, even though you knew at the time that these things happen and that this is a horrible sensation, yet you went ahead and did it anyway and weren't fully conscious and aware of what you were doing. There's the feeling that you don't have enough time to do it and are going to be late. I can't get at the meat of it, at the heart of what makes it feel so terrible. There is also the fact that you don't actually want to do the task at hand and perhaps the most horrible fear is that you're not capable, that it's too hard, although it seems unlikely because you have done that kind of thing before. If you're unmotivated, the task that you're unmotivated to do becomes a horror.

(Pause.)

I will always remember these times.

(Byron blows the candle out.)

END OF PLAY

Groundwork of the Metaphysic of Morals

*For The National Theater of
the United States of America
and Radiohole*

Production History

Groundwork of the Metaphysic of Morals was originally produced by Young Jean Lee's Theater Company. It premiered in July 2003 at the Ontological-Hysteric Theater in New York. The direction, set, costume and sound design were by Young Jean Lee; the lighting design was by Owen Hughes. It was performed by:

FU MANCHU	Thomas Bradshaw
FAH LO SEE	Caroline Kim
SHEILA	Kate E. Ryan
TERRENCE	David Giambusso
STAGE MANAGER	Samuel D. Hunter

Characters

FU MANCHU

FAH LO SEE

SHEILA

TERRENCE

STAGE MANAGER

Intro

The stage is bare except for a crappy-looking, canvas-covered metal screen on wheels off to the side. Behind the screen are all of the performers and props for the show, as well as a stage manager sitting with his back to the audience. The screen is too small to adequately hide them all, so you can see parts of people sticking out. All exits and entrances are made to and from behind this screen. The only furniture used is a small wooden bench large enough for two people and a ridiculously short-legged stool that makes people's knees stick up when they sit on it. The performers bring the furniture on- and offstage with them as indicated in the stage directions. At the rear of the stage are stairs leading up to a balcony. The lights remain up during scene changes.

Sudden blackout.

"Funky Drummer Boy," performed by Thornetta Davis from the album Making Spirits Bright: A Holiday Season with Nordstrom, *begins.*

The lights come up on the first bass note.

The song plays.

The song stops.
Long pause.
Fah Lo See and Fu Manchu enter. They are both wearing the cheapest kind of clothes you can find in Chinatown. Fah Lo See is Asian and wears a red Chinese dress with black Chinese Mary Jane–style shoes. Fu Manchu is black and wears black Chinese pajamas with black karate shoes. The pajamas are too big for him and the sleeves and pants' legs hang down over his hands and feet.
They stare at the audience for a long time.

FAH LO SEE: There's something about white people's faces . . .

(Pause.)

Sometimes I look at you—at that blankness—and think there's no way I could ever hurt you enough.

(They exit.)

Sheila's Father's Study

Sheila enters with the bench, sets it down, and sits. She is Caucasian and wears a glamorous melon-colored pantsuit that ties at the neck.
Pause.
Knocking.

SHEILA: Come in!

(Terrence enters. He is Caucasian and wears a sharp black suit.)

Ah, Terrence.

TERRENCE: Hello, Sheila.

(Long, awkward pause. They have no idea what they're doing Sheila and Terrence exit.)

Fu Manchu's Throne Room

Fu Manchu and Fah Lo See enter with the stool.
Fu Manchu sits on the bench. Fah Lo See puts down the stool and sits on it.

FAH LO SEE: Dad.
FU MANCHU: What, Fah Lo See.
FAH LO SEE: Can you see?
FU MANCHU: Yes.
      Can you see?
FAH LO SEE: No.
FU MANCHU: Open your eyes.
FAH LO SEE: They are open.
FU MANCHU: Are you sure?
FAH LO SEE: Yes.
      What's wrong with me.
FU MANCHU: Nothing.
FAH LO SEE: I think something's wrong with me. I think I'm really fucked-up.

(Pause.)

FU MANCHU *(Singing)*: Bong chong ding dong bing bang bong dang dong.
FAH LO SEE: What does that mean?
FU MANCHU: It means, "The little Chinese men work in the rice paddy."
FAH LO SEE: Why are you singing that to me?
FU MANCHU: I don't know.

(Fu Manchu and Fah Lo See, taking the stool with her, exit.)

Sheila's Father's Study

Sheila and Terrence enter and sit on the bench.

TERRENCE: Sheila, are you happy we're engaged?
SHEILA: Yes.
TERRENCE: Are you happy we live in England?
SHEILA: Yes.
TERRENCE: Are you happy your name is Sheila?
SHEILA: Yes, and I'm happy your name is Terrence and not "Bing Bong Ho" like some Chinaman.

(She laughs. Terrence does not.)

TERRENCE: Are you happy Sir Lionel is your father, and that he's an archaeologist, and that I work for him?
SHEILA: Yes, yes, yes.
TERRENCE: Are you happy your father has been kidnapped and taken to China by Fu Manchu's henchmen after a meeting at the British Museum regarding his expedition to the edge of the Gobi desert, to search for the lost and buried tomb of Genghis Khan, which contains a mask and shield that will enable Fu Manchu to bring together all of the Oriental nations to defeat the West?
SHEILA: No, no.

(Pause.)

TERRENCE: I'm not happy, Sheila.
SHEILA: I know.
TERRENCE: I feel almost hysterical.
SHEILA: Don't be hysterical.

TERRENCE: You said you would help me.

SHEILA: I know I did. I'm sorry.

TERRENCE: I said that I would be perfectly fine with city hall and just our parents and my brother. I said that I would prefer it.

SHEILA: I know.

TERRENCE: But then you said that maybe our friends and family would feel insulted, so we decided that we would do something simple to appease them, and you swore, you *swore* that you would do at least half of this *fucking bullshit* and you haven't. You haven't done anything!

SHEILA: Well, I went to that—

TERRENCE: What, the interview with the goddamned photographer? She came over, Sheila. She came over to the house and you just happened to be there because you were doing something for your father, and you just sat there like a fucking *retard* the whole time saying *nothing*, while I had to bullshit with her for like *two hours* about her artistic vision. Don't even try to talk to me about that interview, you fucking asshole.

SHEILA: I also—

TERRENCE: What? The napkins? I showed you the catalog and you pointed your finger like a fucking retard at the first thing you saw, and it just so happened that they matched.

SHEILA: No, I—

TERRENCE: I can't believe you even dare to speak to me, Sheila. I can't believe you dare to show your face to me.

SHEILA: I'm really sorry, Terrence.

TERRENCE: And you know what makes me the maddest?

SHEILA: You know what, Terrence? I know that I have no right to say anything, and that this is going to make you go completely crazy, but whatever, I have to say it. Yes, I know I completely fucked up and yes, I will try to be better in the future. But I just don't have fucking time for this right now. We're leaving for China tonight to look for that tomb, and I have to get all this shit together, and I'm

sorry, but that's my biggest priority. It just is. I don't know
what else to tell you.

TERRENCE: WHAT?!

(Sheila and Terrence exit.)

Fu Manchu's Throne Room

Fu Manchu, Fah Lo See and Terrence (carrying the stool) enter.
Fu Manchu sits down on the bench. Fah Lo See stands to
one side of Fu Manchu. Terrence puts down the stool on the
other side and sits on it.

FU MANCHU: Look, I have this beautiful daughter.
    Look at my daughter, Terrence.
    Check out my beautiful daughter.
TERRENCE: I don't want to look at her.
FU MANCHU: Good! Now say my name.
TERRENCE: Fu Manchu.
FU MANCHU: Say, "I don't want to look at her, Fu Manchu."
TERRENCE: I don't want to look at her, Fu Manchu.
FU MANCHU: Look at her!

(Pause.)

Say, "No!"
TERRENCE: No!
FU MANCHU: Yes!
TERRENCE: No!
FU MANCHU: Yes!
    Tell me where that tomb is.

(Pause.)

Say, "No!"

TERRENCE: No!

FU MANCHU: Yes!

TERRENCE: No!

FU MANCHU: Yes!

*(Fu Manchu looks at Terrence expectantly.
Long pause.)*

Fuck you!

TERRENCE: Sorry, I'm just tired.

FU MANCHU: I'm tired, too!

*(Fu Manchu, Fah Lo See and Terrence, taking the stool
with him, exit.)*

Sheila's Father's Garden

Sheila and Terrence enter and sit on the bench.

TERRENCE: Sheila . . . I . . .

I love you so much, Sheila. You're the most important
thing to me in the world. I'm completely obsessed with
you.

Sheila, there's no one else like you.

SHEILA: What's wrong with you! Can't you see I don't care
about that right now?

TERRENCE: I'm sorry, Sheila! I was—

SHEILA: Okay, Terrence, this is what I want you to do. We got
the fucking mask and shield, so I want you to take them
and give them to Fu Manchu and don't come back without my father. Do you think you can do that?

TERRENCE: But the coolies—

SHEILA: Fuck that.

TERRENCE: Okay.

SHEILA: Okay. Thanks.

(Sheila and Terrence, taking the bench, exit.)

Fu Manchu's Entertainment Room

*The sound of guests speaking in fake Oriental languages
(made by performers from behind the screen).
Fu Manchu enters and goes up into the balcony.*

FU MANCHU *(To the audience)*: Gentlemen, I would like to
thank you all for coming to my humble home. You have
traveled many miles over long distances to hear what
I am about to say—from Taiwan to Taipei, from Hong
Kong to Beijing. You have traveled from many foreign
different lands—India, Mongolia, Cambodia, Taiwan.
From every different Oriental nation you have come.

Now that you have partaken of some light refreshment,
I would like to delight you with some worthless entertainment.

It is my intense shame and dishonor to present to you
my ugly and insignificant daughter.

*(Fah Lo See enters wearing a large, smiling papier-mâché
Oriental-girl head.*

"Square Dance," performed by Eminem from the album
The Eminem Show, *begins.*

*Fah Lo See does a dance that incorporates martial arts
movements. Fu Manchu enthusiastically shows his love of
rap, making exaggerated rapper motions and screaming
out the rapper's name with joy.*

The song ends.

Fah Lo See comes downstage.)

FAH LO SEE *(To the audience)*: I hate you.

Sometimes when I'm around you my face starts burning and my vision goes blurry because my feeling of

hatred is so intense. Whenever I say, "What?" and pretend I didn't hear what you just said, it's because I'm experiencing this sensation.

I think that you're an idiot. Every time you make a statement in which you attribute some personal characteristic to yourself, I want to kill you.

Maybe you're wondering, "Why does she kiss my ass all the time?" And the answer is I don't know. I don't know why.

Something about being here makes me feel like I have to.

(Fah Lo See exits.
Fu Manchu exits.)

Fu Manchu's Throne Room

Terrence (carrying the stool, a sword and a cheap Chinese mask) and Fu Manchu (carrying the bench) enter. They put down the bench and stool. They sit.

FU MANCHU: Let me see them.

(Terrence hands him the sword and mask.)

They look weird.
TERRENCE: I don't think so.
FU MANCHU: Something's wrong with them.
TERRENCE: I tell you there's nothing wrong.
    I have to go to the bathroom.
FU MANCHU: You can't use the bathroom here. It's broken.
TERRENCE: Then give me Sir Lionel.
FU MANCHU: I can't. He's burning in the furnace. Ha ha.
TERRENCE: That's not funny.
FU MANCHU: Why isn't it.
TERRENCE: He's going to be my father-in-law.

FU MANCHU: How nice.

TERRENCE: I know he's here, crawling around in the dirt.

FU MANCHU: I think I'll test them.

TERRENCE: Test them? With what?

FU MANCHU: My tester.

TERRENCE *(Looking around)*: Where is it?

FU MANCHU *(Exiting)*: In here.

*(Sound of the tester is made by the stage manager.
Fu Manchu's Oriental howl of anguish and rage.
Fu Manchu reenters.)*

You lied.

TERRENCE: I didn't.

FU MANCHU: They're not. They're not real. You lied. I'm going to go to the bathroom.

TERRENCE: I have to go to the bathroom.

FU MANCHU: Don't try to copy me.

TERRENCE: Look, I don't even know where they got those things.

FU MANCHU: Do you think that these people are your friends? They're not. They're an ocean, a vast ocean that contains nothing except for everything.

TERRENCE: I feel so betrayed.

I feel like . . . I feel like someone is trying to kill me.

FU MANCHU: It's all over for you.

TERRENCE: Let me at least try to get some true feeling.

FU MANCHU: Go ahead and try.

(Pause.)

TERRENCE: I feel bad.

FU MANCHU: You think it's that easy, don't you. You think you can just copy someone else and then you can be famous.

TERRENCE: I don't even want to be famous.

FU MANCHU: Your brain is completely fried, Terrence.

TERRENCE: Your face is a pancake.

FU MANCHU: Stop trying to copy me!

TERRENCE: Sorry, I can't help it.

(Terrence, carrying the stool, and Fu Manchu, carrying the bench, sword and mask, exit.)

Fu Manchu's Dungeon

Terrence enters with a rope, sits on the floor, binds his wrists to his ankles, and rolls onto his side, facing the audience.

TERRENCE: There was the day before yesterday when I was talking to Hall-Ramsden from the British Museum and reaching the pinnacle of my dreams that I had worried over so, that the British Museum wasn't responding to my requests, and then everything went so much my way that Hall-Ramsden came with his assistant and everything I didn't do perfectly but I did well and was charming and he seemed to like me although this was a mixed blessing, I must say. Then there was the moment that Ali Mahmoud and I had the exchange about excavating the tomb that made everyone laugh and impressed everyone, including I think Sheila. Then there was the pinnacle moment, the night before last, when Sheila was pounding my back and telling me that she heard my report was excellent and could she see it, which was possibly the happiest moment of my entire life.

Today I will manage to fill the time until bedtime and may self-destruct at some point and not be able to continue doing things that make me sane, and I may start pounding my head against the floor again and listening obsessively for some shred of good news which will never come. And Sheila will be busy plundering the tomb and nobody will give me a thought and I won't come in to work all week and it would have all been avoidable if Nayland had just called me back or if I'd called someone else or if I'd asked Nayland about everything earlier, which I didn't.

I hate everyone.

(Fah Lo See enters and looks at Terrence with painful longing.)

FAH LO SEE *(Uncertainly)*: Hi.

(Pause.)

Terrence?
TERRENCE *(Coldly)*: What.

*(Fah Lo See exits.
Terrence unties himself and exits.)*

Fu Manchu's Throne Room

Fu Manchu (carrying the bench) and Fah Lo See (carrying the stool) enter. They set their shit down. Fu Manchu sits. Fah Lo See stands next to him.

FU MANCHU: We can just kill him no problem.
FAH LO SEE: No.
    Let's drug him.
FU MANCHU: No.
FAH LO SEE: Why not?
FU MANCHU: You don't want to see what he's like when he's on those drugs.

FAH LO SEE: Sure I do.

FU MANCHU: He'll become like a glazed chicken.

FAH LO SEE: I don't care.

FU MANCHU: He'll become a glazed turkey, lying on the platter.

FAH LO SEE: I don't care. I like that.

FU MANCHU: You do?

FAH LO SEE: No. I don't know.

FU MANCHU: What?

FAH LO SEE: I have to go get a turkey baster.

FU MANCHU: Why?

FAH LO SEE: It's Thanksgiving.

FU MANCHU: Let's give thanks for all the good things that we have.

(They bow their heads.)

FAH LO SEE: Dear Lord, I know I haven't spoken to you for a while, and that I'm being sacrilegious right at this moment, but I can't help it, I can't help it, and there is some true feeling here.

FU MANCHU: Let's give him the drugs.

FAH LO SEE: No. I don't want to see what he's like that way.

FU MANCHU: Come on, it'll be funny.

FAH LO SEE: It won't be.

FU MANCHU: We'll make him drink his own pee!

FAH LO SEE: Dad you have a one-track mind.

FU MANCHU: What do you have? An eight-track?

FAH LO SEE: I don't even have a record player, just this crappy radio.

FU MANCHU *(Sagely)*: But you can hear everything anyway.

(Fu Manchu, carrying the bench, and Fah Lo See, carrying the stool, exit.)

Fu Manchu's Dungeon

Terrence enters and stands far downstage with a stupefied look on his face, his eyes rolled back in his head and his mouth hanging open.
  "I'll Be," performed by E. J. Day from the album American Idol: Greatest Moments, *begins.*
  Fah Lo See enters slowly and takes Terrence's hand.
  She looks at the audience unhappily.
  The song ends.
  Fah Lo See and Terrence exit.

The Backyard of Sheila and
Terrence's Rented House in China

Sheila and Terrence (an apple bulging in his pocket) enter. Terrence carries a shovel and sets it against the back wall. He moves downstage center.
  All of Terrence's lines should be said as pretentiously as possible. Sheila uses a weird unidentifiable European accent and speaks very loudly.

TERRENCE: Who am I?
SHEILA: What is my identity?
TERRENCE: When I look into the mirror, am I really seeing myself, or a representation of myself?
SHEILA: Is my body really my body, or an extension of my mind?
TERRENCE: I can feel my body.
SHEILA: I can feel my body, yearning to dance.

> *(Terrence pulls the red apple out of his pocket and begins a pretentious, anguished "Shall I eat the apple / Shall I not eat the apple" dance. Sheila shadows his dance and "interprets" it by making gutteral, vaguely Oriental noises.*
>   *Pause.*
>   *Sheila and Terrence return to their normal selves.)*

I don't want to do this anymore Terrence.
TERRENCE: Why not. It's fun.
SHEILA: It's stupid and mean. What's the point.
TERRENCE: I think it's funny.

(He goes to get the shovel.)

SHEILA: Anyone can do this. What is this? This is nothing.
TERRENCE *(Digging a hole)*: Whatever Sheila.
SHEILA: Tell me what happened to my father.
TERRENCE: I just don't, I don't have anything really to say.
SHEILA: I . . . what are you feeling?
TERRENCE: Nothing nothing nothing.

(He looks into the hole.)

Where is this shit?
SHEILA: Do you, what are you thinking?
TERRENCE: Nothing.
    (Looking into the hole) Where is this shit, Sheila?
Where's the real mask and shield?
SHEILA: I don't know, one of the coolies buried it.

(Terrence continues to dig.)

What is Fu Manchu's house like?
TERRENCE: I don't know, it doesn't matter.

(They exit.)

Fu Manchu's Throne Room

Fu Manchu (carrying the bench) and Sheila (carrying the stool) enter. Fu Manchu sits on the bench and Sheila stands.

SHEILA *(Screaming)*: NOOOOOO!

163

(Sheila falls to the ground, adjusting herself so it looks like every bone in her body is broken.
Pause.
Fu Manchu looks at Sheila, then looks away.
Pause.
Fu Manchu looks at Sheila.
Pause.)

FU MANCHU: I don't know what to say, because I've never experienced anything like this myself before. I don't . . . I know there are things that happen in this world that I have no experience of. I know that sometimes one person gets a nice family and someone else gets a blown-off face.

I'm veering off, always, but what I really want to say is that I'm sorry for not suffering more, for not knowing more of suffering and what it is like in the world.

I don't know how many years I have to wait before someone will tell me where to go and sit and stand and sleep, where I can rest on a stone with my satchel full of books and bread and my little jug of milk, and pray for good things.

I wish that I could be in love. That is what I wish. And it is all so sad, it is all so sad and I can't access the feeling. I can't access the deep sad feeling that will enable me to say what I must say to you, which is look at that canoe in the sky and your father is looking down on you, floating, in his canoe, and he is crying because you are sad, and maybe if you cheer up then he will smile for two seconds and light up the whole sky, and it will be a shooting star.

(Fu Manchu and Sheila exit.)

Fu Manchu's Throne Room

Fah Lo See, Terrence and Sheila enter.
Terrence stands with his arm around Fah Lo See, an idiotic, stupefied look on his face.
Sheila stands facing them.
Pause.
The sound of the tester is made by the stage manager.
Fu Manchu's Oriental cry of joy.
Fu Manchu enters with the sword and mask and sits on the bench.

FU MANCHU: I'm so happy.

(Sheila runs up to Terrence.)

SHEILA: Oh Terry look at me, please look at me. Look! It's your Sheila talking! Now I want you to listen to me and listen to me good. These people have drugged you Terry, oh, you're not yourself.

And here is what I want to tell you. I love you so much, I love you SO MUCH. And even though I might not feel that way most of the time, I want you to know that there is some true feeling here, Terry, and it isn't all bullshit it just isn't. There are depths upon depths here, things too complicated to understand.

Like the idea that love is about judgment, about judging others and yourself on a fixed hierarchical scale and calculating who can best feed your desperation for how long.

It's all so twisted, the way you feel for me, the way Fah Lo See looks into your eyes. And I pity everyone for being trapped like that, for being trapped into this fucking hellhole.

(Pause.)

165

TERRENCE: Bong bong!

(Sheila turns to Fu Manchu.)

SHEILA: You hideous yellow monster!
FAH LO SEE: Don't call my father that!
SHEILA: Fuck you!
FAH LO SEE: Fuck you!
SHEILA: FUCK YOU!
FAH LO SEE: FUCK YOU!
FU MANCHU: Everybody shut the fuck up!
SHEILA AND FAH LO SEE: Fuck you!
FU MANCHU: You are all assholes!
TERRENCE: Bong bong!
FAH LO SEE: Shut up, Terrence!
TERRENCE: Bong bong!

(Fah Lo See attacks Terrence and they fall to the ground.)

FAH LO SEE: I fucking hate you!
FU MANCHU: Don't fight here!
SHEILA *(Awkwardly getting on top of Fah Lo See and Terrence)*:
    Fah Lo See, stop it!
FAH LO SEE: I can do what I want!
TERRENCE *(Struggling under Fah Lo See and Sheila)*: Bong
    bong!
FU MANCHU: I . . . you're all going to die, except Terrence,
    who will get some drugs, and then he'll die when he's
    good and ready! But until then, everyone hang on and see
    what happens!

(Fah Lo See pulls away from them.)

FAH LO SEE: I want to talk about what I'm perceiving right
    at this moment, which is a room full of people who all
    know how to behave except me, and it's not fair!
SHEILA *(Getting up)*: Shut up, Fah Lo See!

FU MANCHU *(To Sheila)*: Why don't you shut up!
SHEILA: Fuck you!
FU MANCHU: Fuck you!
FAH LO SEE: It's not fair!
TERRENCE: Bong bong!
FU MANCHU: Okay!
    I'm going to kill all of the white people now!
TERRENCE: Bong bong!
FAH LO SEE: Can't you ever say anything besides, "Bong bong!" you fucking retard!
TERRENCE: Bong bong!
SHEILA: He's not retarded!
FAH LO SEE: Yes he is!
FU MANCHU: You are all retarded except for my daughter!
SHEILA *(To Fu Manchu)*: *You're* retarded!
TERRENCE: I'm not . . . retarded.
SHEILA: Terry!
FAH LO SEE: Don't touch him!
SHEILA: Fuck you!
FU MANCHU: Fucking retards!

(A loud, extended choking noise is made by the stage manager from behind the screen.
    Everyone remains expressionless.)

Okay, wait.

(The stage manager makes a noise like he's hacking up a chicken wing.
    Everyone exits.)

Fu Manchu's Throne Room

Fah Lo See enters, sits on the bench and looks at the audience.

FAH LO SEE: Everything is fairly clear and straightforward, like on a balcony in bare feet with the stone of the balcony against your face, shot in the back, fallen to the ground with an arrow sticking out of your head.

And I'm sorry to have been such a disappointment to you. I mean that sincerely. But I also feel kind of like, fuck you.

(Fah Lo See exits, taking the bench with her.)

Fu Manchu's Bridal Preparation Chamber

Sheila enters wearing a sheer, white gown over her pantsuit.
She stands on the stool.
Fu Manchu enters.

FU MANCHU: Hello.

(Sheila doesn't answer.)

Do you have to go to the bathroom?
SHEILA: No.
FU MANCHU: Do you like your dress?
SHEILA: No.
FU MANCHU: My bathroom is still broken.
SHEILA: Why do you keep bringing that up? No one cares.
FU MANCHU: It's broken, everyone cares.
SHEILA: You hideous yellow monster.
FU MANCHU: Don't say that.
SHEILA: Why not? It's true isn't it. Your face is all yellow, like a peacock. It's beautiful. It's the most beautiful face I've ever seen.

(Pause.)

FU MANCHU: Do you know why you're wearing that dress?
SHEILA: Yes.
       Why are you in here?
FU MANCHU: I don't know.
SHEILA: You must know something.
FU MANCHU: I had a dream of a pumpkin. The pumpkin was too big and it scared me, and that's all I remember. The dreams were coming out of my skull like bats.
SHEILA: My head is a pumpkin.
FU MANCHU: It is not.
SHEILA: It is too.

(Pause.)

FU MANCHU: I don't know what we're talking about.
SHEILA: I don't either.
FU MANCHU: There is no reason for me to be in here.
SHEILA: Okay.

(Fu Manchu and Sheila, carrying the stool, exit.)

Fu Manchu's Balcony

The sound of wild cheering and stamping from the Oriental masses (made by the performers from behind the screen).
    Fu Manchu enters with the sword and mask and goes up into the balcony.

FU MANCHU: Oriental people! Our time has come!

(The sound of wild cheering and stamping from the Oriental masses.)

With this mask and shield of Genghis Khan, we will come together to defeat all of the Western nations!

(The sound of wild cheering and stamping from the Oriental masses.)

You fucking morons!

(The sound of wild cheering and stamping from the Oriental masses.)

Shut up!

(The sound of the Oriental masses becoming silent.)

All day long, you think about nothing but the most stupid shit! Like idiotic television shows and movies, and how much approval people show you when you talk to them. Your biggest complaint is that you don't get to see yourselves represented in the media as being the opposite of what you in fact are. You have terrible taste in everything, and you constantly go around trying to convince people of how special you are.

You're not special! You're morons! And then when something bad happens I find myself completely alone. And the white people go on laughing and talking as usual while I'm suddenly in the middle of a nightmare. It's like when you're walking through a park on a sunny day, feeling suicidal, and you see people lying on the grass or throwing frisbees, and the images burn themselves into your eyes.

(Pause.
   The sound of wild cheering and stamping from the Oriental masses.)

I hate you!

(The sound of wild cheering and stamping from the Oriental masses that continues as Fu Manchu descends

from the balcony. The cheering becomes a chant of "Fu Manchu! Fu Manchu!" accompanied by stamping and pounding. As Fu Manchu reaches the second to last step, the screen falls down, exposing the stage manager's back and the performers. The stage manager does not move and the performers quickly put the screen back up.)

Fu Manchu's Testing Room

Terrence (with the bench) and Sheila (with the stool) enter. Terrence stands the bench on its side with its legs facing away from the audience. Sheila places the stool on top of it with its legs facing down to form Fu Manchu's "tester."
They look down at an imaginary trap door in the floor.

TERRENCE: What do we do.
SHEILA: I've got an idea. What's this.
TERRENCE: It's a trap door.
SHEILA: I can hear the Orientals shouting nearby.
TERRENCE: Open that door.
SHEILA: Okay.

(She opens it.)

Well look at that.
TERRENCE: Look at that. It opens right up onto the square where Fu Manchu and the Oriental masses are shouting. I can see Fah Lo See.
SHEILA: She's laid out for sacrifice like a turkey on a platter.
TERRENCE: Let's kill them.
SHEILA: Okay.
TERRENCE: Let's fry them and fry them and fry them until they're all dead.
SHEILA: Okay, but how?

TERRENCE *(Walking over to the tester)*: If we redirect these laser beams from Fu Manchu's tester onto the Oriental masses, we can kill them all.

SHEILA: Okay.

(Terrence and Sheila turn the bench around so that its legs face toward the trap door. Terrence flips the stool over so that its legs face upward and he "locks" it into place with a slight twist to form the handles of the Oriental-killing machine.

When the machine is finished, they grasp the handles, aim the machine at the hole in the floor, and shoot.

The sound of the Oriental-killing machine made by the stage manager is accompanied by the sound of Orientals being fried, made by Fu Manchu and Fah Lo See from behind the screen.

The sound stops.

Sheila and Terrence exit.)

Fu Manchu's Testing Room

Sheila and Terrence enter.

Terrence stares into the trap-door opening in the floor while Sheila stands behind him.

SHEILA: We should probably go soon.

(Terrence continues to stare down into the opening.)

Come on, Terrence. Let's get out of here.

TERRENCE: What were they thinking, anyway? Everyone knows that white people are just going to do whatever they want and there's nothing you can do to stop them.

SHEILA: Come on, Terrence.

TERRENCE: Why were they so unhappy?

SHEILA: I don't know.

TERRENCE: Maybe we did something to them. Maybe it was our fault.

SHEILA: Why would it be our fault.

TERRENCE: What if the whole world is a structure that is built up around white people and men controlling everything and being superior. What if everything, including the way we breathe, is structured by this.

SHEILA: There's no such thing as a master structure. It's all just individuals working towards their goals.

TERRENCE: How do you know?

SHEILA: I don't like to think in terms of race. I like to see people as human individuals.

TERRENCE: Huh.

SHEILA: I don't even think there's any such thing as race.

TERRENCE: Huh interesting.

SHEILA: It's based on facts, on historical evidence.

TERRENCE: What about racism?

SHEILA: Slavery was racism, and when you drag a black man behind your truck for mile upon mile.

TERRENCE: Maybe you shouldn't say that.

SHEILA: No! I'm going to fight, because this kind of reverse racism makes me mad! People think I won't stand up for myself, but I will!

TERRENCE: You seem very mad.

SHEILA: I'm going to show everyone that I can make it, that I can succeed without these complaints of racism bringing me down, making me feel bad about myself! I want everything to be fair and nondiscriminatory and based on logic, and fuck you! Everything I think is based on logic! Maybe we should get out of here.

TERRENCE: I would like to stay a minute.

(Sheila exits.)

Orientals, I miss you! Though I know it is probably horrible and racist for me to say this, there was something about your culture that I valued so much. There was your incredible hospitality, and your wonderful food and religion and oh, everything! And I don't understand. I don't understand why we have to shoot and kill each other like this, but I promise I will try to understand better from now on. I accept the theory about everything being an evil structure that makes every breath we take, that makes the very idea of breathing, serve the white man. And I am aware that right at this moment, *right at this moment* I am being evil and disgusting. But I will try and try and try and try, and every day I will try harder to be responsible. I will be responsible.

(Terrence exits.)

The Deck of a Luxury Ocean Liner

Sheila and Terrence enter wearing a formal gown and white tux, respectively, with glasses of champagne. They go up into the balcony.

SHEILA: I feel bad.
TERRENCE: Why?
SHEILA: For killing all of those Chinese people.

(Lights out.)

END OF PLAY

Yaggoo

For Jeffrey M. Jones

Production History

Yaggoo was originally produced by Young Jean Lee's Theater Company. It premiered in June 2003 at Little Theater at Tonic in New York. It was directed and designed by Young Jean Lee and performed by:

WHALER   Jesse Hawley

Whaler stands, facing the audience.

WHALER: Let me list all the ways. Let me list all the wonderful, precious moments.

(Pause.)

And there have been all of these anxious, anxiety-provoking moments too. There was the time I spoke to Captain Hackluyt about my opinions about seasickness and he didn't answer me back or address any of my suggestions at all or use them. There were the three times I spoke to the Captain about little things asking him little questions and he didn't answer me back. There's the fact that Captain Hackluyt was one of the few people on the ship who never, ever tried to talk to me. The other was Yaggoo.

I'm blanking for some reason—usually these pop into my head and cause out loud cursings like on the forecastle when I'm taking snuff. There's yesterday, which made me want to kill myself. There's the fact that I came back to the inn after leaving in triumph the way I was supposed to, to redeem my reputation as a bugger, which I was afraid I was getting, with this stupid, half-true-sounding story about losing my pipe that makes me seem pathetic, and being invited out for dinner through the spyhole by the Captain because the door was locked and nobody was answering my knocks.

Then there's the constantly being sick from seasickness or alcohol. This is bad. This is very, very bad because it's destroying me, probably, and making me feel like crap all the time and probably contributing to my low emotional state.

You see, this is what happens.

You get all pumped up—I was so pumped up from that other night and all that male bonding, and then it all comes crashing down. So this is the key. You don't expect things and hope for them and prepare for them. You just expect nothing, so that when things happen it's a total surprise. Things have to happen naturally, like in my whole boyhood theory of: "Do your duty, without thought for the fruits of your labor," which was I guess a pretty damned good theory although it never worked and seems still like a pretty horrible and dangerous theory.

I remember one time the Captain told me to go work below or abaft, and since I'd already asked about work in the stern and there was none, I went down to where Comstock, the Captain's pet, was. And he was organizing, and I was helping and screwed some stuff up, and then he started ignoring me all awkward, and then Yaggoo came down and stared at us all paranoid, and I asked him for work and he gave me some and I went back up to the deck and it was so humiliating and awkward. And then later I was avoiding Comstock but we made eye contact a few times and I live in horror that he thought I was staring at him or something. My fond hope was that he was looking at me, but that's almost certainly untrue.

But anyway, last night after I went back to the inn I had dinner with the Captain and his men. Everyone was so manly and strong and courageous and socially like that, and I felt quite alienated.

There are all of these subtleties and complexities that I don't have the patience to get into. What compelled me in the past was this pain, this need to confess, this need to describe all of the things that were hurting me in great detail. What I feel now is nothing. I want to go into this coma-like state of pursuing women and planning how to get it and whom to have it with and satisfying my need to have it and then planning how to get rid of it and then starting over.

Okay, okay, okay.

There are many things going on, and I haven't been thinking.

Here I am again sitting on my stool that needs to be fixed but I haven't had time/was too lazy/hungover whatever. The whale tooth is in my lap and I am carving it. I am in front of my window. The weather has changed it is no longer hot and it is getting colder.

How do I reach the tentacles outward from this stool? How did I do it before?

I think I need to go through the entire dinner. I can't remember things perfectly well and I probably can't remember them in order, so I will just remember different things that happened in a rough order.

Yesterday I also sat here in the same place on the same stool with whale teeth and it is the march of days, the same and the same, the day after day, and you go on like that as you get older and then you die. These things are universal, they are obvious. Yesterday I was thinking perhaps so obvious that smart people Captain Hackluyt do not even bother about them because what's the point, but I like to bother about them because they horrify me.

And today I feel that I am bursting, that I am bursting with too many things and I can't get them all out because there are layers to every day, layers and layers of thought and experience that are each dense in their own way and follow their own train of thought, and you have to go back and unpack each one and remember each little jump in thought, and it's all just too much because there's just too much and you're like the skin of something about to explode.

Yesterday I saw good and evil good and evil and the good have this thing, this thing that I could look at and grasp in my hand and say "this is good" even though the world is confusing there is this one thing that is obviously outrightly good.

And that thing is friendship between males.

There were all of the moments in which Scoresby expressed his approval of me and clapped me on the back. There was the moment that Comstock clapped me on the back and then told me to sue him. There was the moment that the Captain invited me to have dinner. There was the moment that Don Pedro smiled at me at the table as if he were really glad to see me and liked me, and all of the subsequent smiles that looked like that, like after the soup, the second after I clapped him on the back, or some other time like before the soup after I'd clapped him on the back before the fish, I think.

Oh, I had an idea last night of getting a completely blunt assessment of where I'm at, and of presenting myself in that way. This is what I am. These are the humiliations. This is what I did, and this is what I am, and here I am, and no apologies. Just whatever, this is how it is.

END OF PLAY

What's Wrong with These Plays?

An Afterword

By Jeffrey M. Jones

> I sat down and thought, "What's the worst possible play I could write—the last kind of play I would ever think about writing." I just thought [writing about the English Romantic poets in *The Appeal*] was such a pretentious, horrible idea for a play and thought it would be interesting to try to write it.
>
> —YOUNG JEAN LEE
> *Brooklyn Rail*, April 2004

There can't be many playwrights who've asked themselves, "What's the worst play I could write?" *and then written that play.* Fewer still would have found success with such a strategy. Young Jean Lee first encountered the technique as a writing exercise in Mac Wellman's Brooklyn College MFA playwriting program. But she's used it for each new play since then (including the six collected here), and, in 2007, received the OBIE's Emerging Playwright Award.

Lee goes on to explain that setting out to write the worst possible play[1] is a way of giving oneself permission to trust one's instincts; to put down whatever comes to mind, bypassing self-censorship. Her process is, in fact, a distillation of her whole vision of theater, an encapsulation of her authorial stance which, at the same time, expresses the purpose of her writing:

> I do this because I've found that the best way to make theater that unsettles and challenges my audience is to do things that make me uncomfortable . . . My work is about struggling to achieve something in the face of failure and incompetence and not-knowing. The discomfort and awkwardness involved in watching this struggle reflects the truth of my experience.

Deliberately writing a "bad" play is also an explicit rejection of the tidiness and aspiration toward uplift and "quality" which characterize so much mainstream American playwriting. In fact, I don't think you can appreciate how good these plays are without understanding how and why they are "bad"—strange and unsettling; perversely defective; deliberately inauthentic. Taken together, they create a Bizarro[2] world of blunders and mistakes, in which everything is either

---

[1] The definition of "worst possible" play has evolved along with Lee herself. What started as a classroom exercise soon became "writing the last play in the world I'd ever want to write" and now "writing the hardest play, the biggest challenge."

[2] The Bizarro world of DC Comics was a recurrent feature in which the elements of the Superman story line were, in every sense, "backwards," i.e., primitive as well as reversed. Bizarro Superman was a villain—an erratic, dull-witted, ham-fisted bruiser who looked like an early version of The Thing. The line art was deliberately clumsy and ugly—the fluid curves of Superman's musculature replaced by angular lumps of some gray, chalky material. All the characters were stupid, and the overall battle of good against evil was continually on the verge of coming undone through the sheer incompetence of the actors on both sides. The point of this exercise, for artists and readers alike, can only have been the surprising pleasure of trashing the all-American imagery of the parent strip.

out-of-whack or missing altogether. It's as if these plays seek
out as many ways as possible to be wrong and to get it wrong.
Therein lies not only their peculiar genius, but the source of
their profound and liberating originality.

What's Wrong with This Character?

It is a truism of the theater that a good play must have well-
rounded, sympathetic and consistent characters; that individual behavior is always motivated; and is therefore ulti-
mately knowable, and therefore can and should be revealed
as a principal outcome of a play.

So you might expect that a book of six different plays
would also contain a cast of widely varied characters in
diverse situations, whose interactions would be meaningful,
and about whom you would be asked to care deeply.

This is not that book.

In Young Jean Lee's plays, most of the characters know
there's something very wrong with them. Take the evil Fah Lo
See, daughter of Fu Manchu, in *Groundwork of the Metaphysic of Morals*:

> FAH LO SEE: What's wrong with me.
> FU MANCHU: Nothing.
> FAH LO SEE: I think something's wrong with me.
> I think I'm really fucked-up.

Or consider the Korean-American, in *Songs of the Dragons
Flying to Heaven*:

> KOREAN-AMERICAN: I walk around all day feeling
> like I have no idea what I'm doing and am mess-
> ing everything up, and I'm constantly tortured
> by the thought that other people can see what an
> idiot I am and hate me for it.

Poets in *The Appeal* have a similar problem. Here's Wordsworth:

> WORDSWORTH: I can't seem to control my mouth or
> body or anything, and something that I'm doing
> is always slightly wrong.

Even Tom, the self-help guru, in *Pullman, WA*, is falling apart:

> TOM *(To the audience)*: I don't know how to live. I don't
> know how to act around other people. I have no
> idea what the fuck I'm doing.

Character after character in play after play is afflicted with
this common condition. Like White Person 2 in *Songs*, they
are deeply agitated, and yet paralyzed by their feelings:

> WHITE PERSON 2: I wake up in the morning with a
> horrible feeling, a horrible dread pushing down
> on me . . . There are so many things I need to do.
> So many things. And I am terrified of them all,
> of each and every single one of them, and I feel
> weak, I feel unequipped to handle any of these
> things, so I want to run away. I want to do some-
> thing that will make me disappear, that will
> make me feel and think nothing other than what-
> ever it is that is making me disappear . . .

Like The Whaler in *Yaggoo*, they're always on the verge of
figuring out what's wrong—yet the immensity of the problem
overwhelms them:

> WHALER: And today I feel that I am bursting, that
> I am bursting with too many things and I can't
> get them all out because there are layers to every
> day, layers and layers of thought and experience

that are each dense in their own way and follow
their own train of thought, and you have to go
back and unpack each one and remember each
little jump in thought, and it's all just too much
because there's just too much and you're like the
skin of something about to explode.

If the characters in these plays find their own experience
hard to comprehend, the thoughts and motives and feelings
of everyone else are completely unknowable to them. Characters in different plays use virtually the same language to
describe poring over the minutiae of recent "moments," trying to figure out what other people were doing and thinking,
always with the desperate hope of winning their respect,
always with the lurking fear that they've inadvertently humiliated themselves:

> WHALER: There was the moment that Don Pedro
> smiled at me at the table as if he were really glad
> to see me and liked me, and all of the subse-
> quent smiles that looked like that, like after the
> soup, the second after I clapped him on the
> back, or some other time like before the soup
> after I'd clapped him on the back before the fish,
> I think . . .

The same idea is expressed by Terrence (in *Groundwork*) and
Byron (in *The Appeal*):

> TERRENCE: Then there was the moment that Ali
> Mahmoud and I had the exchange about exca-
> vating the tomb that made everyone laugh and
> impressed everyone, including I think Sheila . . .

> BYRON: There was the moment when Wordsworth
> smiled at me in the garden as if he were really

glad to see me and liked me, and all of the subsequent smiles that looked like that, like the second day I was there, the day after I flirted with Dorothy in the hills, or some other day like Thursday after I'd flirted with her the week before, I think . . .

It's almost as if everyone else in the world is part of some vast conspiracy:

> FAH LO SEE: I want to talk about what I'm perceiving right at this moment, which is a room full of people who all know how to behave except me, and it's not fair!

Or once again, Byron:

> BYRON: What am I feeling right now? I am panicking because I am afraid that Wordsworth thinks that I am a psychopath asshole loser undesirable person and that everyone is talking about me behind my back and that I am going to be told that my presence is no longer desired.

Sometimes what looks like hostility is just a simple misunderstanding—because other people's behavior is simply bizarre and unsettling:

> DOROTHY: You're a total and complete fucking moron.
> WORDSWORTH: What?
> DOROTHY: What.
> WORDSWORTH: You just said that I was a total and complete fucking moron.
> DOROTHY: Oh. I was talking to myself.
> WORDSWORTH: Oh.

Often, though, the conspiracy is only too real, and other people reveal they're being deliberately deceptive (as in *Songs*):

> WHITE PERSON 1: Let's talk about my inside, my inner private life. When I'm sitting in the room with you, sitting right in front of you, you can see what I'm doing. But the thing is, you don't know what I'm really doing because the second I walk out of this room, you don't have any idea what the fuck I'm doing. I say I'm going to the bathroom, and you can imagine what I would be doing, but what if that's not what I'm doing at all? What if I'm not fucking going to the fucking bathroom? What then?

Sucked into a bottomless maelstrom of apprehension, surrounded by people who all seem to know something they don't, Lee's characters give up, become catatonic, infantilized "retards."[3] They have problems gathering their wits, completing sentences, sustaining a train of thought: "I'm veering off, always," says Fu Manchu. "I'm blanking for some reason," echoes the Whaler. In *Groundwork* (as elsewhere), characters are obsessed with finding their "true feelings" which, for some reason, they "can't access":

> FU MANCHU: It's all over for you.
> TERRENCE: Let me at least try to get some true feeling.
> FU MANCHU: Go ahead and try.
> TERRENCE: I feel bad.

And in another scene:

> SHEILA: And here is what I want to tell you. I love you so much, I love you SO MUCH. And even

---

[3] The word, which appears fourteen times in this volume, is of course a schoolyard term, and conveys not mere stupidity but a total lack of cool.

though I might not feel that way most of the time, I want you to know that there is some true feeling here, Terry, and it isn't all bullshit it just isn't. There are depths upon depths here, things too complicated to understand . . .

And another:

FU MANCHU: I wish that I could be in love. That is what I wish. And it is all so sad, it is all so sad and I can't access the feeling. I can't access the deep sad feeling that will enable me to say what I must say to you . . .

What is missing, above all, is the ability to connect in the moment with another human being in *any* meaningful way. Indeed, there are scenes—the tea party in *The Appeal*, the "alcoholism" exchange in *Dragons*—in which spontaneous human interaction can only be approximated though play-acting, and natural behavior must be rehearsed in order to "get it right."

Lee achieves maximum dissociation with her characterizations of the Romantic poets. I defy anyone to read or watch *The Appeal* without at some point objecting, "But *that* isn't Wordsworth!" Yet who is Wordsworth? Wordsworth himself will tell you, but it won't help:

WORDSWORTH *(Putting down his pen)*: Ah, my poem is finished.
(To the audience) Hi, my name is William Wordsworth. You might have heard of me. I'm one of the poets known as English Romantic. Other Romantic poets include: Blake, Coleridge, Byron, Shelley, and Keats. We all existed in the nineteenth century.

Yet on second thought, this gets to the heart of the matter. If Wordsworth, being dead, exists at all, he exists as the name "Wordsworth" (the play obviously wouldn't work if the characters were named Miller, Smith and Rabinowitz), the name serving as token or "pointer" to a set of attributes and associations we maintain about an historical character. But here is the curious thing: no matter how un-Wordsworthy her Wordsworth becomes, the initial association with "Wordsworth" never completely goes away. The idea of Wordsworth, and specifically that the character exists in some relation to Wordsworth, remains. Lee's Wordsworth, then, both *is and isn't* "Wordsworth." Just as "Wordsworth" is an idea, character—at least in the plays of Young Jean Lee—isn't so much the set of all truths about an individual, as an idea about an individual to which the actual person stands in tenuous ambiguity.

You don't have to be much of an armchair psychologist to read this particular constellation of feelings—that you're a clueless "retard," unable to read other people (who are all somehow better than you, and privy to a secret you will never learn); continually humiliated by your own behavior, yet at the same time dissociated from your feelings; and only tenuously connected to whatever name, role or label others have assigned to you—to relate this to Lee's personal experience as a second-generation Korean-American, raised by evangelical Christians in rural Washington State, who went on to pursue a Ph.D. in English literature from Berkeley before dropping out to write plays in Brooklyn.

If there is an "issue" that crops up throughout these plays, it's racism. *Groundwork* and *Songs* address it head on, but even Lord Byron (in *The Appeal*) has evidently written a poem called "Ching Chong Chinaman," while in *Pullman, WA*, Pete and Tom inexplicably burst out chanting, "Hai, hai, a-fing-a-fong hai, a wikka-wok hai mekka ching-a-chong hai." But once again, Young Jean Lee deliberately "gets it wrong."

What's Wrong with the Asian People?

On the surface, both *Groundwork* and *Songs* would appear to be the antithesis of the conventional "identity-politics" play. Instead of positive images, the plays offer up a steady stream of "politically incorrect" stereotype and invective. Consider the opening lines of *Songs*:

> KOREAN-AMERICAN: Have you ever noticed how most Asian-Americans are slightly brain-damaged from having grown up with Asian parents?
>
> It's like being raised by monkeys—these retarded monkeys who can barely speak English and who are too evil to understand anything besides conformity and status.

The character continues in what appear to be a series of contradictory non sequiturs on Korean-American identity, before abruptly turning on the audience:

> I feel so much pity for you right now.
>
> You have no idea what's going on. The wiliness of the Korean is beyond anything that you could ever hope to imagine.
>
> I can promise you one thing, which is that we will crush you.
>
> You may laugh now, but remember my words when you and your offspring are writhing under our yoke.

At first, it's startling to hear Asians indulge in racist diatribes or call for the elimination of their enemies (as with Fu Manchu: "I'm going to kill all the white people now!"). We're conditioned to expect this from whites, so at first we're caught off-guard (which, of course, is precisely Lee's intention).

Does Lee imply that race relations might somehow stabilize on the basis of mutual loathing and contempt?

Closer examination reveals something much more unsettling. Racism, after all, presupposes that ethnicity and cultural background are absolute determinants of identity and therefore, of one's place in society. But here as elsewhere in Lee's plays, identity itself turns out to be mutable and unreliable. For one thing, the Asians vacillate between submission and defiance. Their Asian identity is sometimes a source of pride, sometimes a source of humiliation. Dominant Asians express contempt for submissive Asians (and clueless whites), while some seem willing to reject their Asian identity altogether to become white. Like whites, they can find reasons to hate themselves which have nothing to do with being Asian. In fact, the distinction between Asian and white frequently disappears in a blur of mutually felt self-loathing. And both sides are depicted with equal parts mockery and sympathy.

Lee demarcates this enormous jumble of racial roles and categories to demonstrate both their persuasiveness and their intricacy. Given such contradictory positions within our culture, it would be facile to expect easy resolution, and, indeed, the prevailing method of these plays is to pose contradiction against contradiction in an endless chain. The slurs are presented without comment, from continually shifting vantage points. The audience is asked to accept racist imagery as entertainment, then accused of being racist, then subjected to racist attack. The point is to keep everything off-balance, by maintaining a state in which neither characters nor audience is really sure of what is going on. As Young Jean Lee herself has said:

> I'm just trying to transplant the confused jumble of racial stuff in my head into the audience's head so that they're forced to think about it and be disturbed by it in a way that they wouldn't be if I were trying to preach some message at them. I want them to recog-

nize contradictory aspects of themselves and explore their own reactions and motives. I just want to make them think, and come to their own conclusions.

In the end, however, the balance is asymmetric. While the Asians' racism is ferociously antagonistic, white racism is typically off-hand and casual. It's just not a big deal. And the fates of whites and Asians couldn't be more different: in *Groundwork*, the Asians are wiped out by a death ray, while Sheila and Terrence, on the deck of an ocean liner, "feel bad for killing all of those Chinese people." In *Songs*, the Koreans mime a series of suicides, then literally bow out in a unison chorus, which ends with the stereotypic: "I apologize for bringing shame upon my country." The play continues for several more pages, but the White People, poring over relationship issues, never even notice they're gone.

What's Wrong with These Plays?

We've come a long way from the notion that the action of a play should, as much as possible, happen in a single location in something approximating real time. But we still expect Chekhov's rifle to go off in the third act, and, by extension, that anything an author puts in the play is there for a reason which will become apparent by play's end, because *the end is defined as the place where everything gets tied up*.

Today we expect, in the name of representational authenticity, that characters will behave "like themselves" over the course of the play; that the patterns of dramatic action will appear shaped into regular structures; that extraneous detail will not be introduced; that one thing will lead to another in a plausible way; that what happens in one spot will not contradict what has happened in another; that the events and narratives shown in the play will bear some relation to what the play "is about" and so forth.

These are all assumptions that Young Jean Lee challenges, subverts, discards and reinvents, and the plays in this volume represent an unusually detailed record of her systematic deconstruction of dramatic structure. *Yaggoo* at first glance appears to be what Beckett called "a piece of monologue," wherein a lone voice in a static and attenuated landscape broods over past events. But however abstracted Beckett's plays may be, there's never a suggestion that his narrators are themselves unreliable, or that the events remembered never actually happened. As the so-called "Whaler's" memories accumulate, on the other hand, they seem increasingly contrived. What on earth, is happening here:

> WHALER: There's the fact that I came back to the inn
> after leaving in triumph the way I was supposed
> to, to redeem my reputation as a bugger, which
> I was afraid I was getting, with this stupid, half-
> true-sounding story about losing my pipe that
> makes me seem pathetic, and being invited out
> for dinner through the spyhole by the Captain
> because the door was locked and nobody was
> answering my knocks.

Is the Captain (whom the Whaler has previously told us "never ever tried to talk to me") on the other side of a locked door, speaking through a "spyhole," inviting him to dinner? For that matter, try piecing together what actually happened at the inn—are we to understand the Whaler left in triumph (in itself an implausibility) and then returned, with a pathetic story, in order to *redeem his reputation as a bugger*?

The man performs any number of "whalerly" actions, like carving scrimshaw, without being terribly convincing. He's more like a whaler in a theme park, where all the supposedly authentic activities are, in fact, staged. For that matter, why "whaler" in the first place? And if the events of the story line are murky, what about the events of the play as they unfold in real time? What, to be specific, *happens* in *Yaggoo*? One is tempted to say, almost nothing, really. A Whaler—who admits: "I can't remember things perfectly well and I probably can't remember them in order, so I will just remember different things that happened in a rough order"—remembers things. He experiences a welter of feelings and memories of feelings—to no cumulative effect—a continual shift of focus and context, subject and tone, leading nowhere. Not exactly dramaturgy as it's usually taught.

The plays that follow chronologically (*Groundwork* and *The Appeal*) provide more in the way of story and situation, but in neither case do these traditional elements ground the plays in actuality or provide the foundation of their meaning. The invocation of "bad theater" further undercuts the framework of situation and plot. We are reminded throughout that the world of the play is immaterial and bogus, as when Terrence ties himself up onstage to indicate that he is being held prisoner; or a screen falls down to reveal "offstage" performers creating sound effects, which were obviously fake in any case; or when Wordsworth steps out of character to introduce the Romantic Poets, or mimes going fishing. The sequence of scenes becomes increasingly arbitrary and irregular. Characters no longer speak with a consistent voice or tone, and continuity begins to break down even within the dialogue itself. What little "forward action" exists is dissipated by digressions, non sequiturs, jokey wordplay, schoolyard infantilism, or even random, hammy acting. Sometimes the characters themselves simply give up the pretense of action entirely and walk away from the scene, as here in *Groundwork*:

FU MANCHU: I don't know what we're talking about.
SHEILA: I don't either.
FU MANCHU: There is no reason for me to be in here.
SHEILA: Okay.

(Fu Manchu and Sheila, carrying stool, exit.)

Lee's later plays—*Pullman, WA*; *Church* and *Songs*—are increasingly presentational: not so much plays, in the conventional sense, as structured events, which purportedly happen in real time. The characters are the performers themselves, and the action—no longer confined behind a fourth wall within the context of a story—takes place directly with the audience. Dramaturgy, freed of the freight of meaning, now creates patterns from an assortment of elements which may or may not have connections with each other.

Pullman, WA, for example, has an almost mathematical structure, in which three speakers take turns, alternating between inspirational and aggressive diatribes that range over several sets of stock themes and images (Christian/Biblical, self-actualizing, romantic/fantastic, etc.). The specifics at any given moment (i.e., of speaker, subject, imagery and tone) seem almost arbitrary, even as the fluctuations in tone, intention, speaker and imagery attain a kind of regularity.

Church is the logical culmination (to date) of Lee's reinvention of dramatic form. Though it feels like the most seamless of the six plays, it is actually composed of the most disparate elements—scenes interspersed with songs and dances, capped by a final chorale, structured as an actual event (i.e., a church service happening in real time). The relationship between performers and audience is especially clear, as is the reason for the presentation: the characters of the play want to bring the audience to God. Though the play is nonnarrative, it is full of stories, often very strange ones, invoking mummies, "trees made of water and fish made of birds and all manner of unimaginable-looking things." Yet curiously, it no longer matters whether the words themselves are plausible. A sufficient degree of plausibility—a *kind* of authenticity—is generated simply by having a performer tell a story matter-of-factly:

REVEREND WEENA: This is my testimony. Once
upon a time I was bad and did drugs in every

color of the rainbow. Blue and purple and brown and gold, and I took them all at once and washed them down with whiskey. And I was in my bathrobe, and then I smoked some pot.

Then I found some prostitutes and did sin with them, and then I found some pipes and banged the prostitutes on the head, and it was good. And then I wandered through the gutter where there were some chickens lying around and I stuck the pipes right through them so that the blood gushed upwards like a fountain, and I stuck my mouth over the pipe and let the blood gush upwards into my mouth and lift me up into the sky. And I was raised about ten feet into the air by this gushing tower of chicken blood, and I didn't care. I was floating and free.

Lee in effect has extended her handling of historical "truth" to the issue of faith. Just as she sidestepped the problem of authenticity by assigning the name "Wordsworth" to a hodge-podge of behaviors and associations which variously were and were not "like" any actual Wordsworth, so here she side-steps the problem of faith by presenting implausible events as the testimony of a true believer. Barring some weird mir-acle of voodoo, Weena's story cannot possibly be true. Yet because theater is, after all, an act of collective belief, it doesn't matter. It is possible to entertain her statements as truthful as long as the play itself presents them as truthful. The play veers continually from sincerity to absurdity, with straightforward sermons followed by surreal imagery fol-lowed by heartfelt song or prayer, until the categories of truth and falsehood are swallowed up within an infectious cele-bration of the joys of selfless love. For *Church*, the least ironic of Lee's plays, turns out to be a surprisingly powerful demon-stration of the thesis misattributed to Tertullian: *credo quia absurdum* ("I believe because it is absurd."), and raises for the first time the only possible alternative to the crazy confusion of the world—the crazy possibility of hope.

What's Wrong with the World into Which We Were Born?

One does not, as a rule, expect theology south of 14th Street. Yet if the cumulative effect of these six plays is a picture of a world gone seriously wrong, Lee's yearning for a higher resolution is found in their concluding moments, which taken together suggest a path of spiritual awakening.

Yaggoo, Lee's first play, admits of little more than the possibility of coming to terms with an ugly truth:

> WHALER: This is what I am. These are the humiliations. This is what I did, and this is what I am, and here I am, and no apologies. Just whatever, this is how it is.

Groundwork ends on a perfunctory note of remorse ("I feel bad." "Why?" "For killing all of those Chinese people.") while *The Appeal* concludes with elegiac regret:

> BYRON: Then there is this horrible, nightmarish sensation that comes when you realize how much you have to do and how all of the time you had to do it in has been squandered by you yet again, even though you knew at the time that these things happen and that this is a horrible sensation, yet you went ahead and did it anyway and weren't fully conscious and aware of what you were doing . . . I will always remember these times.

But her three later plays end with dreams. *Pullman, WA* offers only a nightmare of hacked-up mermaid body parts:

TORY: There were mountains of mermaid-tail fish
   slices and mermaid torsos planted like bushes
   all around. Mermaid guts hung from all the trees
   and the lakes were clogged with mermaid hair.
   The fields were littered with squirming mermaid
   babies who lay unattended as hundreds of frolicking mermaids played kickball with hundreds
   of mermaid heads.
   As I walked to my waiting rainbow coach,
   squashing a mermaid baby head with each step,
   I realized how fortunate I truly am.

Cold comfort, indeed: hell as painted by Hieronymus Bosch.
Yet in *Songs of the Dragons*, what starts as satire—the white
cloud which leads to couples counseling, detox and personal
fulfillment—suddenly shifts to the sublime:

WHITE PERSON 1: And I dreamed . . . that suddenly
   the world opened up before us and many of our
   bad feelings went away. I dreamed that we
   learned how to be humble and realistic, and that
   our newfound humility enabled us to develop
   our true gifts to a greater extent than we could
   when we were beating ourselves up to do better.
   I dreamed that we both stopped hating ourselves
   enough to value each other's love and look after
   it, and that we grew old together, and had grandchildren, and children, and things like that. It
   was the most wonderful dream I've ever had.

Here, as if for the first time, we find a vision of the peaceable
kingdom, a heaven on earth, achievable with humility and
love. True, the moment is immediately undercut ("It doesn't
have to just be a dream! It can be true! We can call up one of
our friends and ask them for the name of a therapist."). But

Church takes the pursuit of "how to live" to its most complex expression, in the concluding parable.

The story is framed in Old Testament terms—rival brothers, dutiful servant—but ends squarely in the New Testament—death, resurrection, the prospect of eternity in paradise in the presence of Jesus:

> REVEREND JOSÉ: And suddenly Jesus himself was there, and the delight she knew thereafter is not ours to comprehend until death.

And then, the last word:

Hallelujah.

In the world of downtown New York theater, that's as wrong as it gets.

JEFFREY M. JONES is a playwright and essayist. He is the author of *70 Scenes of Halloween*; *Nightcoil*; a series of collage plays (*Der Inka Von Peru*, *Tomorrowland* and *Wipeout*); a series of *Crazy Plays*; *Stone Monkey Banished* (an adaptation of *Monkey* for Ralph Lee); *12 Brothers* (an adaptation of the Brothers Grimm tale, with Camila Jones); and two musicals: *Write If You Get Work* (score by Dan Moses Schreier) and *J. P. Morgan Saves the Nation* (score by Jonathan Larson). His plays are published by Broadway Play Publishing and Sun & Moon Press. He has been manager of The Wooster Group, Richard Foreman and John Jesurun and has taught playwriting at the Yale School of Drama. He is currently co-curator of the OBIE-winning Little Theatre series at Dixon Place. His blogsite is http://jeffreymjones.blogspot.com.

YOUNG JEAN LEE was born in Korea in 1974 and moved to the United States when she was two. She grew up in Pullman, WA, and attended college at UC Berkeley, where she majored in English. Immediately after college, she entered Berkeley's English Ph.D. program, where she studied Shakespeare for six years before dropping out and moving to New York in 2002 to make theater. Since then, she has directed her plays throughout the U.S. and Europe. She is a member of New Dramatists and 13P, and has an MFA from Mac Wellman's playwriting program at Brooklyn College. She is the recipient of the OBIE's Emerging Playwright Award and is the artistic director of Young Jean Lee's Theater Company (www. youngjeanlee.org).